Advanced Praise for *Truth Telling in a Post-Truth World*

"I love reading Steve Long. He's not only smart, funny, and well-informed but also wise. He sees farther then puts all the pieces of the pattern together in a way I couldn't have foreseen. His work shows that theology can be again what it once was—truthful, wise, even joyful and delightful."
—**Jason Byassee**, Vancouver School of Theology

"Steve Long has the uncanny ability to propose (in language the nonspecialist can readily understand) a depth of theological, philosophical, and political theory. I have some theoretical disagreements, but I have learned much from this important book and hope that it convinces many thoughtful readers to recognize the priority of truth over power in our public and political life."
—**Charles E. Curran**, Perkins School of Theology, Southern Methodist University

"This is a book of profound wisdom with transformative potential if read and taken to heart in churches throughout the United States. Stephen Long offers a powerful theological analysis of this perilous moment in American political life, where moral cynicism has replaced the search for truth and goodness. Long warns us of the dangers of the drift toward a post-truth society that has lost its moral bearings as politics deteriorates into a battle for power within an adversarial system. This book is a clarion call to churches and Christians to keep alive the question of truth, and that the quest for justice is one that should be heeded."
—**Richard D. Crane**, Messiah College

D. Stephen Long

TRUTH TELLING
IN A POST-

TRUTH WORLD

Truth Telling in a Post-Truth World

The General Board of Higher Education and Ministry leads and serves The United Methodist Church in the recruitment, preparation, nurture, education, and support of Christian leaders—lay and clergy—for the work of making disciples of Jesus Christ for the transformation of the world. The General Board of Higher Education and Ministry of The United Methodist Church serves as an advocate for the intellectual life of the church. The Board's mission embodies the Wesleyan tradition of commitment to the education of laypersons and ordained persons by providing access to higher education for all persons.

Wesley's Foundery Books is an imprint of the General Board of Higher Education and Ministry, The United Methodist Church, and named for the abandoned foundery that early followers of John Wesley transformed, which became the cradle of London's Methodist movement.

GHBEM Publishing is an affiliate member of the Association of University Presses.

Truth Telling in a Post-Truth World

All web addresses were correct and operational at the time of publication.

ISBN 978-1-945935-50-3

Manufactured in the United States of America

HIGHER EDUCATION & MINISTRY
General Board of Higher Education and Ministry
THE UNITED METHODIST CHURCH

For Harper Ann Joyce

CONTENTS

PREFACE

I had not planned on writing this book. Having just finished a work titled *Augustinian and Ecclesial Christian Ethics: On Loving Enemies*, I had decided to turn my attention to the infused virtues of charity, faith, and hope for a volume tentatively titled *Infusing Virtue*. Then I received an invitation from the General Board of Higher Education and Ministry of The United Methodist Church to write a book on truth in a post-truth culture. I had written several short pieces on this topic and presented lectures on it but had not anticipated putting together a volume on truth. I was honored to be asked by my church to do this and decided to do it as a discharge of my role as an ordained United Methodist elder. So I agreed but said it would take me until 2020 at the earliest to put it together. However, given what is occurring in the US context, and now globally, the project seemed more pressing and urgent, so I set everything aside and put together what I hope is an accessible work that considers our cultural context and appropriate theological, philosophical, and political responses within it. I am deeply grateful to Matthew Charlton and Kathy Armistead for the invitation. I have written enough books to know that they seldom have the kind of influence to change things an author desires, but if this work is a contribution to a better cultural and political discourse in any sense, it will have been worth it. At least my grandchildren will know that I tried.

Several people read portions of the manuscript. Jason Byassee and Stanley Hauerwas encouraged me to see the project through. I asked three people whose counsel has always meant a great deal to me to read it and help me to make it fit the times in which we live. My parents, Wayne and Sue Long, and my wife, Ricka, did so, making important suggestions and giving me wise counsel for how to think and live in these days. Justin Bronson Barringer read through the entire work with an attentiveness that strengthened it immensely. His care for this project humbled me. He dared to tell me the truth, making the comment on an early draft: "This is the most boring chapter conclusion in the history of chapter conclusions. Please end with something better." I have been honored to have colleagues like Justin in my life. I am in his debt, and so will you be, dear reader, if you invest the time and energy necessary to read this work and it does not bore you. He made it livelier and more coherent than it otherwise would have been.

The year in which I worked on this manuscript was a blessed one for my family. We welcomed our first grandchild—Harper Ann Joyce. She has been a source of delight and an object of holy curiosity as we watch her develop and grow before our eyes, renewing, strengthening, and broadening relationships. Patient readers who see their way to the end of this book will discover that it emphasizes not only the virtue of truth telling but also the importance of courage, justice, charity, faith, and hope. These virtues generate the conditions that allow us to receive new life with joy, a moral endeavor if ever there was one.

Most of this material is previously unpublished. Part of the conclusion to chapter 4 came from "Redeeming the Curse of Work through Charity," in *Catalyst*, May 8, 2017.[1] The section "Money, Truth, and Political Speech" was originally a white paper with that same title in *Lo$ing Our Faith in Our Democracy,* Auburn

---

1 D. Stephen Long, "Redeeming the Curse of Work through Charity: A Maximum Moral Income," *Catalyst*, May 8, 2010, http://www .catalystresources.org/redeeming-the-curse-of-work-through-charity-a -maximum-moral-income/.

Seminary, October 2013.[2] I am grateful for the permission to use those pieces here. Christopher B. Barnett and Clark J. Elliston invited me to be part of a project on "Martin Scorsese as Theologian." The section "Nihilism and the Marketplace" was originally written for that project.

---

2 Auburn Seminary, *Lo$ing Faith in Our Democracy: A Theological Critique of the Role of Money in Politics*, Auburn Applied Theology Series, vol. 1 (October 2013), https://auburnseminary.org/report/losing-faith/.

INTRODUCTION

Where would we be without the truth telling
of Socrates, Jesus, Martin Luther King Jr.,
John Brown, and countless others?

The presidential election of 2016 marks a significant moment in US politics, culture, and church life, but why it is significant is not yet clear given the diverse explanations for that election.

First, for many on the political left, the election is a symptom, not a cause; it is the logical consequence of cultural trajectories long in place. Here, however, the Left differs. For mainstream progressives, Trump is the logical consequence of the GOP and the conservative movement. For those with a more socialist bent, the movement of which it is the logical consequence is broader, including not only conservatives but also the Democratic National Committee (DNC) and most progressives. Trumpism results from the plutocratic takeover of the two-party system that has abandoned working people at least since the Clinton administration, if it ever served them.

Second, some conservatives view Trumpism as a cause more than a symptom. Trump individually "hijacked" the GOP by falsely presenting himself as a conservative. The conservative movement is not to blame; Trumpist populism is. Trump's previous life as a Democrat and his ignorance of the history of the conservative movement show that he is something unique.

Third, for many in the white evangelical Christian churches, Trump is a gift from God along the lines of Cyrus in the Old Testament (see 2 Chronicles 36:22–23). Just as God raised up an outside, foreign leader to save Israel from Babylonian captivity, so God raised up Trump to restore religious freedom in America, the freedom not to bake a cake for gay weddings, not to be taxed for artificial contraception and abortion, the freedom to pray at public events, and so forth. They may not like much about him, but he is the person God brought to bring something that is being lost in the US.

Fourth, Trump represents the triumph of the business class against the establishment politicians who were ensconced in Washington. We needed a businessman in the White House, and for the first time, we got one.

This book addresses the underlying sickness of our time and its symptoms—an abandonment of the virtue of truth telling and the conditions that might help it flourish.

These four interpretations of the events of 2016 exist in different quarters of the US citizenry. Although they might appear to conflict, they could all be true. The events of 2016 might very well be a symptom of long-standing trajectories and at the same time something new, taking them in a hitherto unknown direction. Nothing prevents something from being both a symptom and a cause. Theologically, Trump might be a "Cyrus" God raised up for judgment, but those who think they are persecuted Israel and Trump is their deliverer may discover they are more in solidarity with Babylon, and what he delivers them into may be even less to their liking. Those who worked to get a businessman in the White House got what they deserved. All four might be true, albeit in ways that we do not yet recognize.

The following work is not about Trump; it is about truth. There are many books already available on Trump from all four perspectives noted above. I have no desire to contribute yet another one, although I will need to refer to him and the movement that makes his work possible, which is what I mean by "Trumpism," and why philosophical and theological discussions of truth should be taken out of the dusty recesses of libraries and placed back at the center of our common life. I prefer the term *Trumpism* because it indicates a movement broader than that of a unique personality who created something new. "Trumpism" signifies that the events of 2016 were both symptom and cause.

Trumpism brings the question of truth and its relationship to politics, culture, and faith to a head. This question can no longer be ignored. As Bob Woodward has documented, Trumpism represents a "war on truth."[1] In the following work, I hope to corroborate that judgment but also to place it within a theological and philosophical context.

> **Trumpism brings the question of truth and its relationship to politics, culture, and faith to a head.**

The first chapter examines why truth matters for politics, culture, and faith. It draws on Plato and Scripture to make a case for truth, especially Jesus's claim in John 8 that the truth will set us free. The central concern of this work is the question, Can we still affirm that truth is a condition for freedom, or has it been replaced? I begin chapter 1 by arguing not only that we can affirm truth but that if we are to have a politics that liberates, we must. Otherwise, despotism, tyranny, and political violence are our most likely future.

The second chapter examines what may have replaced truth as a condition for everyday life—power. It asks if power, absent truth, can set us free. Trumpism, so I shall argue, is a consequence of trying to make power the condition of freedom. It won't work, and I'm fearful that post-Trump, our society will fail to reconsider the attempt to generate freedom from power rather than truth. Power as the condition for freedom is becoming too baked in to who we have become.

Chapter 3 delves more deeply into the conditions for freedom, asking how they relate to the modern nation-state, civil society, and the church. It suggests a fivefold diagnosis for the conditions

---

1 See Bob Woodward, *Fear: Trump in the White House* (New York: Simon and Schuster, 2018).

that gave rise to Trumpism, suggesting that he is both a symptom and a cause. It concludes by arguing that freedom requires truth, and truth requires transparency and accountability. Of course, what remains to be done in a book on truth is to answer, as best one can, Pilate's question, "What is truth?" We can no longer afford to ask that question just to walk away from it.

The conclusion, the fourth chapter, seeks an answer to what truth is and the conditions for a retrieval of the virtue of truth telling.

I fear, however, that this work might be interpreted as reactive, presuming that if the events of 2016 had not transpired, there would be no reason for such a book. I would say two things to counter this possible interpretation: First, the question of truth and its relation to politics, economics, ethics, and theology has been a long-standing concern for me. Two decades ago I published two works suggesting that to understand the world rightly required interpreting it in terms of truth, goodness, and beauty, and that when we lose those predicates, "value" and "power" are prone to dominate our social life. The first work concerned theology and the market, and the second, theology and the social order.[2] After those two works, I realized that I had appealed to truth's importance without a significant engagement as to what truth is. A decade later I attempted to attend to that lack in a work titled *Speaking of God: Theology, Language and Truth*.[3] When I received the honor of being appointed to the Maguire Chair in Ethics at Southern Methodist University, the public lecture I gave on that occasion was "Will the Truth Set You Free in a Post-Truth Political World?" The first line of that lecture stated, "I am tempted to make this a very short lecture and say, 'No.' Any questions?" The world as it is did not, and does not, seem to support an affirmative answer. The temptation to reject any correlation between

---

2   D. Stephen Long, *Divine Economy: Theology and the Market* (London: Routledge, 2000); D. Stephen Long, *The Goodness of God: Theology, the Church and the Social Order* (Grand Rapids, MI: Brazos, 2001).

3   D. Stephen Long, *Speaking of God: Theology, Language, and Truth* (Grand Rapids, MI: Eerdmans, 2009).

truth and freedom is real. When it seems as if those who eschew truth for power are the ones who can maximize their freedom, control leadership positions, gain enormous wealth, and decide what truth will be, then to affirm that truth is a condition for freedom is no easy task. This is why it has preoccupied me for several decades. Because this has been a longtime concern, I read the emergence of Trumpism within those previous works. If I have done so rightly or wrongly is for the reader to decide.

Second, I don't think that this work should be understood primarily as a reaction to Trump because the issues it treats will be as pressing when Trump leaves office as when he occupied it. As long as he is in office, the question of truth is unavoidable. It has become a preoccupation with journalists, politicians, clergy, and laity. It should have been so before, but we had become comfortable with deceptions. Trump at least brings back our discomfort. Once he is removed, whether it occurs through the Twenty-Fifth Amendment, impeachment, election, or term limit, then we may just get back to business as usual, having learned very little from the significant events that have transpired. After the first effort at imposing a Muslim ban, there was a protestor holding a sign at an airport that read, "If Hillary had been elected, we would be at brunch now." My daughter pointed this out to me and said, "And that is the problem." I agree.

As I finish a draft of this work, Donald Trump remains president of the United States. An official in his administration has come forward anonymously (and, I would add, cowardly) to tell the "truth" that many around Trump know: he is incompetent and a danger to democracy, and they are doing what they can to protect the nation. I place "truth" in scare quotes because this telling holds forth little to no possibility of accountability, and therefore it is more like the Supreme Court *Citizens United* decision, which designates corporations as persons with the right to speak with no public accountability. The virtue of truth telling requires agents who can be held accountable.

I have no idea where the US will be by the time this work is published. Perhaps Trump will have been impeached or shown to be in collusion with the Russians; possibly, vindicated from all wrongdoing, he will be on his way to reelection. If this moment passes and business as usual returns and we have learned nothing about ourselves, we will have done nothing more than mask the symptoms without diagnosing the causes. Rather than making Trump a scapegoat upon which we can foist all the faults of US society, these events should cause us to pause and ask, Are we all, to some degree, any degree, complicit? Have we contributed to the susceptibility to the lie? Have we done what we could or should have done to foster the virtue of truth telling? I don't mean to minimize the roles of those who are most directly responsible for Trumpism. They should be held accountable. But without attending to these questions, then breathing a sigh of relief at Trump's passing will only allow whatever has caused the symptom to continue to fester. The following work is an attempt to address one aspect of what I think might be the underlying sickness that has given rise to the symptom—an abandonment of the virtue of truth telling and the conditions that might help it flourish.

WHY SHOULD TRUTH MATTER?

We have arrived at a place in US culture and society in which we are increasingly susceptible to the lie. A major US newspaper tracks and documents the deceptions, mistruths, and outright lies of the US president, and many, especially many who call themselves Christians, either do not care or are willing to look the other way. Bringing attention to that fact might strike some readers as suggesting from the get-go that this work is partisan. That will be for the reader to decide, but it is not my intention. The bold deceits emanating from the Trump White House are the responsibility of Trump and his administration, and they should be held accountable.

Nonetheless, susceptibility to the lie did not emerge overnight. It is not the fault of one person; no one has that kind of power over others. This work, then, is not (I hope) simply a partisan attack on the Trump GOP. It will be obvious to the reader that I find the Trump GOP and what it represents for US society and the Christian church to be deeply troubling. I need to own that from the beginning. I find much of our current political situation unbearable. Children, including infants, are separated from their parents for a misdemeanor. The hatred and fear of refugees, Muslims, and Jews are palpable. White supremacy has been so emboldened that it no longer hides in the shadows, and the political and the ecclesial response has been tepid.

1

I fear that what Trumpism has unleashed might define our political future—demagoguery and open deceit are effective in mass mobilization, and politics in the twenty-first century is first and foremost about mass mobilization. Because politics is about mass mobilization, it too easily becomes preoccupied with power and manipulation. Politicians, political movements, individual citizens, police, those entrusted with the means of violence for the sake of security, perhaps even corporations, athletic teams, universities, and more, will come to the realization that power and advantage matter more in our society than truth. If so, freedom is endangered. Trump's successful run for the presidency and his execution of it show us that the "advantage of the stronger" is more basic to society than justice, that questioning "What is truth?" is more persuasive than the difficult task of discerning truth. Perhaps the greatest casualty of Trump's ascendancy will be the virtue of truth telling. It no longer matters. The crisis we face, however, is not only indebted to Trump. It is part of a larger story, one that exceeds the Trump GOP as well as the US.

The larger story is an old story. It is one of becoming susceptible to, and comfortable with, deceit. Here is a good place to begin:

> Now the serpent was more crafty than any other wild animal that the LORD God had made. He said to the woman, "Did God say, 'You shall not eat from any tree in the garden'?" The woman said to the serpent, "We may eat of the fruit of the trees in the garden; but God said, 'You shall not eat of the fruit of the tree that is in the middle of the garden, nor shall you touch it, or you shall die.'" But the serpent said to the woman, "You will not die; for God knows that when you eat of it your eyes will be opened, and you will be like God, knowing good and evil." (Genesis 3:1–5)

Susceptibility to the Lie

Genesis 3:1–5 offers insight as to why are we so susceptible to the lie, quickly becoming comfortable with it, finding ways to make it palatable, believable, even compelling. The serpent is a crafty liar; he does not outright lie, not in the beginning. People don't tend to believe an outright lie, at least not at first. To get someone to believe an outright lie you must first twist the truth ever so slightly. The serpent begins subtly: "Did God say, 'You shall not eat from any tree in the garden'?" The father of lies knows that the words he utters are not exactly what God said; they have been slightly altered. What God said, as the woman reminds him, was more specific: don't eat from the tree in the middle of the garden. But in slightly twisting the divine word, the crafty serpent sows a seed of doubt in Eve's mind. What was it that God said, and why did God say it? If the fruit can be eaten from most of the trees in the garden, why not this one? What could possibly be wrong with it, especially when it is the tree of the knowledge of good and evil? God would not keep such knowledge from creatures. Having sowed doubt, the father of lies takes our mother Eve one step further, implying that God is the one who has lied, and done so out of envy. God is keeping what is truly good from his creatures, keeping them in the dark because God wants it for himself. God is not to be trusted. Now comes the outright lie: "You will not die." They eat. They die. The lie leads to death. It does every time because deceit and violence go hand in hand.

On February 5, 2003, Colin Powell gave a compelling speech before the United Nations convincing its members that Saddam Hussein was a danger to the international political order for two reasons: First, he was connected to Al-Qaeda through Abu Musab al-Zarqawi. Second, he had weapons of mass destruction. Powell's careful, convincing argument made a case for war against Iraq that led to costly wars that continue to haunt international politics through death and displacement of human life, creating a refugee crisis second only to the one that occurred in the aftermath of World War II. Powell had bipartisan trust. He was known as a man of integrity. What he said was false, although he most likely believed it. The problem, Powell later noted, was that the intelligence was faulty. Hussein was not connected to Al-Qaeda through al-Zarqawi, and there were no weapons of mass destruction.[1] But

---

1   Jason M. Breslow, "Colin Powell: UN Speech 'Was a Great Intelligence Failure,'" *Frontline,* May 17, 2016, https://www.pbs.org/wgbh/frontline

there were powerful forces that wanted him and us to believe the lie, to make us comfortable with it. The politics of the lie is often comforting, telling us what we are already inclined to believe.

Lies work because we become accustomed to minor deceptions.

Falsehoods have convincing power because they have precedents that have prepared the way. Lies work because we become accustomed to minor deceptions. Little lies, lies that might seem less consequential than Powell's, prepare us to be more and more comfortable with outright lies.

Before Powell was Bill Clinton (among others). On January 26, 1998, Clinton went on the national news and denied that he had had an affair with then White House intern Monica Lewinsky. In an impassioned speech, he looked intently into the camera, pointed his finger for rhetorical effect, and with convincing sincerity emphatically stated: "But I want to say one thing to the American people. I want you to listen to me. I'm going to say this again. I did not have sexual relations with that woman. I never told anybody to lie, not a single time, never. These allegations are false, and I need to go back to work for the American people."[2] Later he admitted that he was lying. He was good at it. Many people believed him, and others thought that for the sake of progressive politics, it was best to look the other way. He took some responsibility for it, paid some consequences, but it did not prevent him from maintaining his position as one of the most powerful human beings on the planet.

The lie, of course, is not only found among politicians. It is present throughout culture, society, business, sport, religion, the university; it is present in the family and among friends. Lance

---

/article/colin-powell-u-n-speech-was-a-great-intelligence-failure/.

2 "Bill Clinton: 'I Did Not Have Sexual Relations with That Woman,'" *Washington Post*, online video clip, https://www.washingtonpost.com /video/politics/bill-clinton-i-did-not-have-sexual-relations-with-that -woman/2018/01/25/4a953c22-0221-11e8-86b9-8908743c79dd_video .html?utm_term=.9a6dea97cb91.

Armstrong was a compelling liar, repeatedly stating, "I can emphatically say, I'm not on drugs." Then there was Bernie Madoff, Tyco Inc., Enron, Arthur Andersen, Bear Stearns, Deutsche Bank, Barclays, and many more. The church, of course, is no exception. Televangelists have gone to jail only to be reinstated to their previous positions of power. Clerical sexual abuse is made possible because of the lie. The notorious cover-ups generate other lies. Lovers lie to each other. Friends betray friends. And there are the small lies that persistently bombard us through advertising, manipulating us to desire products even as we know that those products will not deliver on their false promises.

A tradition of lies begets other lies, and truth becomes suspect, prompting us to question, "Is there such a thing as truth?" "How would we know it?" Those questions seem reasonable; their consequences do not. Mike Leach, the head football coach of Washington State University, intentionally doctored a video of Barack Obama for political reasons, and when he was called out, his first response was, "Prove it." When someone did, showing that he had intentionally misled by doctoring the facts, he then responded, "What is a fact?"[3] Washington State University—which touts its "tradition of service to society" and gave us the legendary journalist Edward R. Murrow, who took on McCarthyism—refused to speak for truth and challenge Leach. The academy, where truth should be hallowed, is silent when its highest-paid staff member—the well-paid football coach—questions truth.

> **A tradition of lies begets other lies, and truth becomes suspect.**

How is it that we get caught up in the lie? Mike Leach's question, "What is a fact?" in the face of demonstrable evidence also

---

3   Timothy Egan, "Trickle Down Trumpsters and the Debasement of Language," *New York Times*, June 22, 2018, https://www.nytimes.com/2018/06/22/opinion/trump-leach-lies-language.html?action=click&pgtype=Homepage&clickSource=story-heading&module=opinion-c-col-left-region&region=opinion-c-col-left-region&WT.nav=opinion-c-col-left-region.

did not come from nothing. It, too, had a precedent. As a loyal Trump supporter, he was following a script that had been prepared for him, and one he knew would work. He could question factual evidence and assert an intentional deception because we have become comfortable with the lie, so comfortable that there will be no consequences for its most blatant expressions. A fascinating interview between Kellyanne Conway, counselor to President Donald Trump, and Chuck Todd, reporter for NBC's *Meet the Press,* soon after Trump's inauguration offers a telling glimpse into that script and how the lie gains hold, leading to bizarre and perplexing forms of speech that intentionally miscommunicate.

The context for the interview was a minor disagreement about the crowd size at Trump's inauguration. It was important to Trump that he had the largest crowd ever, but the press continued to report that the crowd was smaller than for previous presidents. Infuriated by this, he sent his press secretary, Sean Spicer, to hold a press conference and set things straight. On January 21, 2017, Spicer went before the press and stated that photographs of the crowds at the inauguration were intentionally framed to "minimize" the crowd size. He then stated, "This was the largest audience to ever witness an inauguration, period, both in person and around the globe." The following day, January 22, 2017, Kellyanne Conway and Chuck Todd held their now infamous exchange that led her to claim that Spicer was not lying but using "alternative facts." Here is a transcript of their exchange:

> **Todd:** Why did the president send out his press secretary, . . . why put him out there for the very first time in front of that podium to utter a provable falsehood? . . .
>
> **Conway:** Chuck, if we are going to keep referring to our press secretary in those types of terms, I think that we are going to have to rethink our relationship here. . . . What happens almost immediately, a falsehood is told about removing the bust of Martin Luther King Jr. from the Oval Office, and that is just flat-out false.
>
> . . .

Todd: . . . you did not answer the question.

Conway: I did answer the question.

Todd: You did not answer the question of why the president asked the White House press secretary to come out in front of the podium for the first time and utter a falsehood. . . .

Conway: Don't be so overly dramatic about it, Chuck. You're saying it's a falsehood, and they're giving Sean Spicer, our press secretary, gave alternative facts to that, but the point remains [*sic*].

Todd: Wait a minute. Alternative facts? Four of the five facts he uttered were just not true. Look, alternative facts are not facts. They are falsehoods.

Conway: Chuck, do you think it's a fact or not that millions of people have lost their plans or health insurance and their doctors under President Obama? . . .

Todd: You sent the press secretary out there to utter a falsehood on the smallest, pettiest thing.

Conway: I don't think anyone can prove, maybe this is me, a pollster, Chuck—and you know data well—I don't think you can prove those numbers one way or another. There is no way to quantify crowds. We all know that.

Todd: *Laughter.*

Conway: You can laugh at me all you want.

Todd: I'm not laughing. I'm just befuddled.

Conway: You are, and I think it's actually symbolic of the way we are treated by the press. I'll just ignore it. I'm bigger than that. I'm a kind and gracious person.[4]

---

4   NBC News, "Kellyanne Conway: Press Secretary Sean Spicer Gave 'Alternative Facts,'" *Meet the Press*, online video clip, January 22, 2017, https://www.youtube.com/watch?v=VSrEEDQgFc8.

This exchange says a great deal about how we become susceptible to the lie. As I previously noted, the first step in making us susceptible to the lie is confusion. What was really said? Was it what you thought you heard? Perhaps it is all a misunderstanding. Second, there is deflection. Once confusion, or befuddlement, gets hold of our communication, then the object about which we are communicating is unclear. Are we discussing falsehood in general? Then why not discuss the media's falsehood about the bust of Dr. King? Why be so selective?

The first step in making us susceptible to the lie is confusion. The second step is deflection. The third step is substituting data for facts.

Consider the case of Colin Kaepernick. Are we discussing police and judicial violence against black Americans, or are we discussing respecting veterans? Confusion and deflection prevent communication. Some of it appears to be willful, some of it not.

A third step in our susceptibility to the lie, and one we will return to in later chapters, is the role of "data." We don't have evidence or fact but, rather, "data," and it will require interpretation. This need for interpretation is the most charitable reading of Conway's claim that Spicer presented "alternative facts." Data is not fact until it is interpreted. Interpretation is never innocent; it serves some political interest. The consequence is that truth, then, can always be questioned: "What is truth?" The question is not really a question; it contains its own answer. Truth can always be put into question through these steps—confusion, deflection, the reduction of things in the world to data, and the assumption that interpretation of the data will always serve someone's political interests.

Yet, when truth is put into question, communication is thwarted, and the possibility of rational discourse disappears. The purpose of language is to communicate. Communication generates communion, a participation in one another's lives by means of the gift of language, one of God's greatest creations. Without the communication of language, there is no communion, no communication, no knowledge, justice, or truth. Yet language does not always achieve its purpose. Much of the above exchange is unintelligible. Its point is neither to communicate nor to clarify but to obfuscate. The term *alternative facts* is the most telling, but notice how "fact" is both affirmed and denied. First it is denied because truth is elusive. Spicer, according to Conway, was not dissembling because there are no certain methods of measuring crowd size. The data is inconclusive. He was giving "alternative facts" that can neither be true nor false. Todd names "alternative facts" as "falsehoods." Conway rejects this accusation. She does not respond to Todd's query about falsehoods but gives him other "facts" that assume agreement between them on what the facts might be. Truth both is and is not at the same time, and, as we shall see, such a claim works against the very definition of what truth is. When it is to her advantage, Conway appeals to the truth of the matter. When it does not, she questions if there is any truth to the matter.

Todd and Conway's exchange, immediately after Trump's inauguration, may be symptomatic of truth's status in US culture. The question "What is truth?" resonates with large swathes of people, but this should give us no comfort. Instead, the power this question has over us puts us in a long tradition of politicians and philosophers who taught us to be skeptical of truth and challenged those who thought it mattered for a good life. Perhaps it is time to take stock and realize that to ask that question and assume no answer is possible puts one in a tradition that includes persons like Thucydides, Pilate, and Nietzsche.

> Asking "What is truth?" is necessary in a free society.

Questioning truth has a long pedigree. Its role in justice, goodness, wisdom, and faith has been challenged from many different angles, having significant consequences for our understanding of politics (truth and justice), goodness (truth and ethics), wisdom (truth and education), and religious life (truth and faith). Pilate joined a list of many when he was confronted with a political and religious truth and took solace in the difficulty we have knowing what it is. "What is truth?" he asked. We will return to Pilate in the next chapter. His take on truth is important to understanding how ancient the politics of the lie is. It was not invented by the Trump administration. In fact, Trump is not a good liar; his lies lack subtlety. Take a minute and compare one of Trump's obvious lies to Clinton's. Clinton is a better liar because he hides his lies well.[5] Trump's lies—and the *Washington Post* has tallied more than five thousand "false or misleading statements" as of October 1, 2018—are blatant and obvious.[6] His presidency represents exactly what Conway said it would, which is in one sense the liar's paradox. It notes that when someone asserts, "I am lying," they assert a paradox. If they are telling the truth, they are lying, and if they are lying they are telling the truth. Conway's "alternative facts" signal that the Trump administration will lie when he and his administration state, "I'm just telling the truth, telling it like it is, but I do so by giving you alternative facts." The obviousness of the lie and its constant repetition draws its listeners in, making them complicit both in the deceit and in the tacit assumption that truth asks too much of us anyway, so why bother? These alternative facts trade on one of the most difficult aspects of truth. How do you know when you have it? Conway questions Todd on the nature of truth—Can we really know it? If there is no certitude by way of the data, we cannot decide one way or another. No one really knows who had the largest crowd. Because we cannot know, nothing we say can be called a falsehood.

It is easier to explain why we are readily susceptible to the lie than it is to explain why telling the truth matters. That will require

---

5   Compare these two videos: "Wolf Blitzer, 'President Trump's False-hoods vs. Lies,'" CNN, June 15, 2018, https://www.youtube.com/watch?v=XLDiXs17-HU; and "Bill Clinton, 'I Did Not Have Sexual Relations with That Woman,'" Miller Center for Public Affairs, Universtiy of Virginia, April 18, 2012, https://www.youtube.com/watch?v=VBe_guezGGc.

6   "President Trump Has Made 4,713 False or Misleading Claims in 592 Days," *Washington Post*, September 4, 2018, https://www.washington post.com/politics/2018/09/04/president-trump-has-made-false-or -misleading-claims-days/?utm_term=.ab1ba644d1a1.

us to discuss what "truth" is, a discussion that will occur in the conclusion to this work. Before we can address that difficult question, however, something more basic is necessary. Why might truth matter for our everyday life? If we find our post-truth culture problematic (as I do), the first step is to convince our friends, neighbors, enemies, and even ourselves, that truth matters. If we could lose truth, and I will argue below that it is so basic to our existence that it cannot ultimately be lost, then we would not

> Explaining why we are susceptible to the lie is easier than saying why truth matters.

even be able to lie. We may have nothing left but "bullshit." The philosopher Harry Frankfurt has argued that there is a distinction between lying and bullshitting. In his essay *On Bullshit* he describes the distinction this way:

> It is impossible for someone to lie unless he thinks he knows the truth. Producing bullshit requires no such conviction. A person who lies is thereby responding to the truth, and he is to that extent respectful of it. When an honest man speaks, he says only what he believes to be true; and for the liar, it is correspondingly indispensable that he considers his statements to be false. For the bullshitter, however, all these bets are off: he is neither on the side of the true nor on the side of the false. His eye is not on the facts at all, as the eyes of the honest man and of the liar are, except insofar as they may be pertinent to his interest in getting away with what he says.[7]

Our post-truth politics fits well with Frankfurt's claim about bullshitting; this should be alarming because the liar might be restored to truth telling, whereas the bullshitter has given up on it altogether. Yet both the bullshitter and the liar have lost the virtue of truth telling and need somehow to find their way back to it. To help trace

---

7   Harry Frankfurt, *On Bullshit* (Princeton, NJ: Princeton University Press, 2005), 55. I am grateful to Brian Volck for reminding me of this important point.

that way back, let us examine some important moments in our philosophical and religious history that show us why truth matters.

The Truth Will Set You Free

The lie is dangerous, but it can never be all that we have, for truth is always more basic than the lie. This claim is metaphysical, theological, and moral. Metaphysics concerns the question of being, of what is. It is metaphysical because our very existence, our "being," is unintelligible apart from truth. Theology concerns the question of who God is. It is theological because the source of that metaphysical claim is that God is, in God's own being, truth and goodness, who in giving us existence cannot but communicate that truth and goodness. Morality concerns the question of goodness. The claim is moral because even though truth is metaphysically and theologically basic, human creatures have the freedom to deny it; and we often do so for immoral reasons. Truth telling does not come easy for us. It is a habit that we must cultivate, just as lying is a vice to which we are easily accustomed. Yet, even the outright lie works only as a parody of truth, thereby witnessing to it.

Truth is more powerful than the lie because God is truth.

Truth is more powerful than the lie because God is truth; one of the names for God in Christian tradition is "the First Truth." In the act of creating, God shares truth. To be and to know that one is, is already to find one's self participating in truth. Creatures could not be without truth, which is why many philosophical and theological traditions correlate being and truth. In the final chapter, we will examine Aristotle's famous definition of truth—"To say of what is that it is, or of what is not that it is not, is true." Truth is what is. To be is to exist in truth because if you truly doubted that you are, that you exist, you could not be present to doubt your own presence. St. Augustine made that claim to counter the skeptics of his day. Their skepticism was predicated upon the more basic truth that they existed and could not reasonably be skeptical about it. There are self-evident truths available to every person, such as something cannot be and not be at the same time. This metaphysical account of truth may seem abstract, but it is very practical. It is one reason we quickly learn not to jump into the path of a moving vehicle. We know that it exists and that it cannot exist and not exist at the same time. We also know that two objects, a moving vehicle and a human body, cannot be in the same time in the same place. No one should experiment with these truths to determine if they are true! Some basic truths are unavoidable. To deny them, or treat them with skepticism, might be something philosophers do hypothetically or for entertainment, but no one can deny them in everyday life without adverse consequences. Truth is basic. The lie is a parasite or a virus on it. It lives off the host of the truth.

> **Truth is basic.
> The lie is a
> parasite on it.**

If truth is so basic, why does the lie seem to defeat it so regularly? The prayer of the Psalmist seems to ring true in nearly every generation: Why do the wicked prosper and the righteous suffer? (see Psalms 73). Prosperity, as the Psalmist notes, is less a sign of God's reward and more a sign that all is not as it should be because too often the wicked speak against heaven, strut through the earth, question divine wisdom, and yet are always at ease, increasing in riches. It makes the Psalmist wonder if God is good to the upright and pure in heart. Why is it that the lie works, that it is effective?

No single answer to that question exists, but the lie takes hold when there is no underlying society to support its importance. In the next section, I will present three scenes that depict the centrality of the truth for a good society. The first is Plato's just city and the need for a philosopher-king. The second is the Jewish Torah and the role of Moses as prophet, priest, and king, and the third is Jesus's proclamation that he is the truth, a truth that is the founding of society and his rule as priest-king. What brings these three scenes together is the assumption that truth is not simply a matter of individual will. If we seek truth, we will need a society ordered to it. Each of these scenes shows how difficult that can be. The point of these scenes is to remind the reader that the questions before us—the questions of truth, falsehood, alternative facts, and power—are not new or unique to us. While the past never identically repeats itself, we have been in similar places before. We begin by looking for how those who came before us addressed the question of what it takes to have a truthful society.

Why Philosopher-Welders Matter

During one debate in the 2015 presidential GOP primary, Senator Marco Rubio made a disparaging comment about philosophy. He should have known better. After all, his own failed candidacy was one more casualty of the deceits played out before a watching public that reduced him to "little Marco." The power of insult was more persuasive than the pursuit of wisdom, deceits more powerful than truth. The art of the deal more compelling than deliberating about goodness. Philosophy, at its best, pursues wisdom, seeks truth, and deliberates about what is good. It is practiced in the university by professional philosophers, but it is also present in the welder's shop when a welder asks a question about the purposes for her or his craft, purposes that would require something more than advantage and power. If people assume that power is all we have, then philosophers who seek to discover something more will be viewed as a threat. They, too, must be disparaged. Rather than challenging this disparagement, Rubio played right into it, saying: "Welders make more money than philosophers. We need more welders and less philosophers."[8]

It is interesting that, like Conway, Rubio's comparison assumes a quantitative assessment of value; it is reduced to data that can be quantified. Conway argued that there was no reliable quantitative measure for crowd sizes, so "alternative facts" about them were possible. Rubio's argument for welders rather than philosophers has a simple criterion for determining value—who makes the most money? Donald Trump used the same criterion during a campaign rally in Minnesota when he asked why other people are

---

8   Alex Leary, "Rubio's No Longer Making Fun of Philosophy Majors," *Tampa Bay Times*, April 4, 2018, http://www.tampabay.com/florida-politics/buzz/2018/04/04/rubios-no-longer-making-fun-of-philosophy-majors/.

called the "elite," even though he has a "better apartment" and more money than they do. He went on, "I became president and they didn't."[9] Here again we find a simple quantitative assessment of value. In stark contrast to the Psalmist's suspicion of wealth, here the person who holds wealth and power is the one who should be given the higher value.

One of the reasons that we are where we are is because we have replaced truth and goodness with "value." More will be said on this in the chapters to come, but suffice it for now to say that value assumes the world is nothing but inert matter without meaning until our will works on it. Once it does, then it has value. Once this becomes the ruling idea, which it has become in politics, business, and some modern philosophy, then the pursuit of wisdom will be abandoned and finally forgotten. No one needs to know anything about the past if all there is is value. Read the first chapter of Donald Trump's *The Art of the Deal*. It is nothing but the record of his day planner. It moves from paragraph to paragraph without any coherent narrative structure. Deal-making is about discrete, unrelated events that are given meaning only through the force of his will. There is no history, no biography, no situating his life within something larger. He begins

> **We lose truth when we become people with no history.**

with "I": "I don't do it for the money. I've got enough, much more than I'll ever need. I do it to do it."[10] Trump is the quintessential modern person, an "I" who appears from nowhere who just "does it." How ironic that his opening line is so similar to Nike's slogan— "Just do it." Of course, no athlete "just does it." To be an excellent athlete takes years of dedicated work, the wisdom of coaches,

---

9   Harriet Agerholm, "Donald Trump Asks Why Other People Are Called the Elite When 'I Have a Much Better Apartment and I Am Richer Than They Are,'" *Independent*, June 21, 2018, https://www.independentco .uk/news/world/americas/donald-trump-elite-better-apartment-richer -minnesota-rally-a8409621.html.

10 Donald Trump, *The Art of the Deal* (New York: Ballantine, 1987), 1.

committed teammates, and more than a little luck. Many debts are incurred along the way. No one says, "I want to run a sub-four-minute mile—I think I'll just do it." Likewise, no one creates wealth simply from the force of his own "I."

Unlike the modern "I," truth will always have a history. It will recognize the debts we owe to those who come before us. We lose truth when we become a people with no history. We lose truth when we choose leaders who lack any historical sensibility as well. In a post-truth culture of alternative facts, it benefits those who would rule for the citizenry not to be well-educated in the humanities—history, philosophy, theology. These disciplines are concerned with the pursuit of truth and wisdom. They remind us of our debts. They are also disappearing in favor of disciplines based on quantitative assessments founded upon the ahistorical, modern "I," disciplines that are replacing a philosophical and theological heritage that seeks truth. Let me offer a too-simple analogy. The university for which I work has as its motto "*Veritas liberabit vos.*" If you asked administrators, faculty, or students what the motto is, however, few if any would say "*Veritas liberabit vos.*" One reason for this is that few read Latin today. Classics departments have disappeared. Few people would know that the motto says, "The truth will set you free." A second reason is our lack of theological knowledge. Even if someone could make out the Latin, they may not know that this motto comes from Scripture, John 8:32, or be able to provide the theological context within which to interpret it. A third reason, and the most important one, is that this motto does not sell; it will not provide what universities need to be sustained today—donors, students, grants. Our university still has this Latin statement as its motto, and it is found throughout the university's architecture. It is residually present, but the motto has been replaced by a more relevant advertising slogan, "World Changers Shaped Here."

Comparing those two statements says a great deal about the status of truth in our culture. The first assumes that truth is to be discovered. Truth, along with beauty and goodness, are present in the world, and a good education seeks to discover them; in discovering them one will find freedom. For this quest, we would need to listen to the past and hear from wise people, some of whom were philosophers and theologians. The second assumes that the world is less a grand mystery effused with truth, goodness, and beauty and more a brute substance that we should endeavor to mold and change as we see fit through the power of our will. The former assumes a person who has a history. The latter needs only an "I" who is willing to "do it." We shape students who shape the world. It is future-oriented, a "modern" endeavor where the modern is understood to be the *modo*, the Latin term from which we get the word "modern" that is best translated as "now." The *modo* is the "now" that is about to arrive and for which we are always ill prepared. Everything that we have done up to this point does not prepare us for it. We must be willing to discard the past for the sake of the *modo* that is always coming but never here.

If this is our world, and I think it is, then it comes as no surprise that welders are viewed as more important than philosophers because welders literally shape the future through their activity. To Rubio's credit, since that debacle of a debate, he has changed his mind, arguing that we need both philosophers and welders. Perhaps he came to realize, albeit too late, that the humanities matter. Logic, evidence, reason, virtue, truth, goodness are worthy pursuits, more so than power, wealth, and a luxurious apartment, even if the former have little "data" on their side. But this is not to disparage welders. They too are necessary. If we are to have a society based on truth, perhaps we don't need just welders and philosophers but welders who are philosophers. If so, we could begin to have a society something like Plato envisioned in his *Republic*. Why would welders need philosophy?

Philosophy is the love of wisdom, and without wisdom we will not know how to distinguish truth from falsehood or goodness from evil. These are not easy tasks, and there are always power brokers who are willing to play up their difficulties for the sake of gaining, wielding, and maintaining power. If welders (and others) are to be responsible members of society, knowing the distinction between truth and falsehood is essential. Why would philosophers need skills at welding? Of course, not every philosopher needs the practical skills of the welder, but the wisdom philosophy seeks will make no difference if it is not put into practice. Philosophy often focuses on theoretical wisdom or contemplation. It is possible for someone to possess it without knowing when and how to use it in a concrete situation. Welders know how to make and fix things. Practical wisdom brings theory to bear on actually existing matters; it helps us understand what should be made and why. A just society, as Plato knew, requires this wisdom. Those who seek wisdom must be the ones who lead. Those who lead must be the ones who seek wisdom. Without it, tyranny can rule. Both philosophers and welders must have the skills to distinguish a true and good politics from despotism, especially if we are not to be led by an aristocratic elite who alone know the truth and convey it to us. Plato argued that we need such an aristocratic elite. He feared that democracy too easily passed over into tyranny because those in power were willing to manipulate the masses by power and advantage rather than draw them together through goodness and truth.

Philosopher-Kings

Rubio could have benefited from a careful reading of Plato's *Republic*. He might have found a description of what he was up against in his debates with Trump in book IX, for it depicts what worries Plato—a ruler who eschews philosophy and surrounds himself with flatterers who obey his every word; someone whose only concern is "victory." Plato wrote during a difficult time. He was an Athenian citizen and observed the people of Athens putting his teacher Socrates to death for unjust reasons. Athens had been defeated in the Peloponnesian War, which lasted from 431 to 404 BCE. Athens led the Delian League, and Sparta led the Peloponnesian League. Athens had been the major city-state in ancient Greece, but Sparta was a powerful oligarchic power. When Sparta defeated Athens, they installed a government of thirty who became known as the "thirty tyrants." They were brutal, killing many, confiscating property, and upending the customs of Athens. Their rule only lasted eight months, but living through it made a lasting impression on Plato. It caused him to consider how tyrants come to rule. One of his answers, and the one most important to us, was that philosophy and political power were divided. Political power primarily pursues what Alasdair MacIntyre calls "the goods of effectiveness."[11] Philosophy pursues "the goods of excellence." If truth is based solely on the goods of effectiveness, then the kinds of quantitative assessments Conway, Rubio, and Trump noted above as determining value will be the dominant factors for a society's self-understanding. Data matters most. If truth is based on the goods of excellence, then that something is effective does not necessarily make it good or true. Effectiveness must be in service to what is excellent. But here is the problem. Most people want effectiveness more so than excellence, and that means they will prefer power to truth.

> **Most people want effectiveness more than excellence, which means they prefer power to truth.**

Thucydides was a contemporary of Plato and was a historian who wrote a book on the Peloponnesian War. His considerations differed from Plato's because he concluded that social, cultural, and political relations are primarily determined by power. People are not moved by reason, by what is true or good, but by power. If this is true, it will have dire consequences for society. There would be no reason to assume that pursuing justice is preferable to pursuing injustice. If justice is nothing but the "advantage of the stronger," then manipulation, coercion, and power will constitute societal norms. Likewise, truth will not set anyone free. It is irrelevant. Seeking power and advantage makes for freedom, at least for the freedom that is possible for those who seek and gain power and advantage. Freedom is to assert one's will without anyone having the power to push back. It is to "do it" and have no one who can stand in your way.

Plato's *Republic* is his response to Thucydides. It begins with Socrates and Glaucon traveling to the city of Piraeus to offer prayers. This setting for *The Republic* is significant because

---

11 Alasdair MacIntyre, *Whose Justice? Which Rationality?* (Notre Dame, IN: University of Notre Dame Press, 1988), 34–46.

Piraeus was the source of resistance to the thirty tyrants. While Socrates and his companions are on their journey, Polemarchus sends his servant to stop them by force. Polemarchus states, "Well, you must prove either stronger than we are, or you will have to stay here."[12] Socrates responds, "Isn't there another alternative, namely, that we persuade you to let us go?" This early exchange sets the stage for the ongoing dispute between Socrates and his interlocutors: What is justice? How is it related to truth, to power? By forcing a dialogue on justice through the threat of violence, Polemarchus demonstrates from the beginning that he does not understand what justice is. He and Socrates go back and forth trying to clarify justice. For instance, Polemarchus interprets justice in a very standard way as giving what you owe to each person to whom it is due. Socrates asks for more clarity, and Polemarchus suggests that we owe good to our friends and harm to our enemies. Socrates finds this inadequate and says: "Justice seems to be some sort of craft of stealing, one that benefits friends and harms enemies. Isn't that what you mean?"[13] Thrasymachus listens to Socrates return each of Polemarchus's answers with a question and finally has had enough. We are told that he wanted to "take over" the argument but had been "restrained" until now. Then, Plato writes, "He coiled himself up like a wild beast about to spring." He tells Socrates it is easy to ask questions but wants him to give an answer—"And don't tell me that it's the right, the beneficial, the probable, the gainful, or the advantageous, but tell me clearly and exactly what you mean."[14] But Socrates does not give him an answer, and Thrasymachus is too impatient for one anyway. Instead, he tells Socrates what justice is: "Justice is nothing other than the advantage of the stronger."[15] Because justice is nothing but the advantage of the stronger, the kind of government that orders society is irrelevant. No matter how they justify themselves,

---

12 Plato, *The Republic,* in Plato, *Complete Works,* ed. John M. Cooper (Indianapolis and Cambridge: Hackett, 1997), 973 or 327c.

13 Plato, *The Republic,* 979.

14 Plato, *The Republic,* 336b.

15 Plato, *The Republic,* 338c.

governments are all engaged in the same activity. Thrasymachus then says, "Don't you know that some cities are ruled by a tyranny, some by a democracy, and some by an aristocracy?" He continues by stating that each makes laws "to its own advantage."[16] If this is what justice is, it bears no relation to what is true or good. It will only bear a relation to winning or profit, and Plato saw firsthand how that opens the door to tyranny. To counter it, he imagined a different kind of city.

Plato's long and "incomplete" argument in *The Republic* is that a just city requires harmony among its parts.[17] The just city mirrors the just soul; both need to be in harmony if power is to be in service to what is true. The soul of the human being consists of three parts: (1) the deliberate, rational part; (2) the spirited, passionate part; and (3) irrational appetites. The last two should serve the former if a person is to be whole and virtuous. Likewise, the city needs a harmony of its three parts—the aristocratic ruler-guardians as the deliberative part, the auxiliaries (from whose ranks the guardians come) as the spirited, and the producers or money makers as the irrational.[18] Plato affirmed aristocracy because he feared that democracy is easily manipulated by demagogues, eventually capitulating to tyranny. It was just such manipulation that led to the death of Socrates and the rise of the thirty tyrants. He favored an aristocracy of the virtuous few, who could provide some restraint against democracy being turned into a mob manipulated by demagogues. What the aristocrats contributed was wisdom. They would rule as philosopher-kings, he wrote: "Until philosophers rule as kings or those who are now called kings and leading men genuinely and adequately philosophize, that is, until political power and philosophy coincide, while the many natures who at present pursue either one exclusively or are forcibly prevented from doing so, cities will have no rest from evils, . . . nor,

---

16 Plato, *The Republic*, 338d.
17 MacIntyre refers to Plato's *Republic* as "a radically incomplete book" (*Whose Justice? Which Rationality?* 82).
18 Plato, *The Republic*, 1072.

I think, will the human race."[19] Political power by itself cannot generate justice, peace, goodness, or truth. Plato's aristocratic society was to combine philosophy's love of truth with the exercise of political power through the person of the philosopher-king. The true philosophers, he stated, are "those who love the sight of truth" and "reach the beautiful itself."[20] Philosopher-kings should rule.

> **Political power by itself cannot generate justice, peace, goodness, or truth.**

Plato's imaginative construction of a just society uniting truth and power has significant limitations. He put forth some extreme ideas about what was needed to create this society. Both women and property should be held in common. To make sure that people are content with their place in society, a "noble lie" should be told to them—a religious myth about how the various classes that make up the city were formed from different metals of the earth for specific purposes. Religion keeps everyone in their place. The imagined city cannot come into being by beginning with the current generation because they are already too determined by partialities that prevent harmony, so to initiate this just society everyone over ten would need to be removed. Plato's *Republic* is indeed "radically incomplete." It is at best an ideal society that some refer to as the "politics of perfection." If only we had the right structures in place, then we could get the perfection of the soul and the city, but the means to get those right structures in place are so horrendous that implementing them would be catastrophic.

Plato's analysis of power and truth far exceeds his solution. His solution does not mark the way forward for a truthful society, yet we have much to learn from his analysis. First, if power does not coincide with truth, its exercise can easily be turned to demagoguery and tyranny. We often hear, and rightly so, that we do not elect a pastor or saint but a president. That is undoubtedly true. We should not expect sainthood from anyone who seeks to

---

19 Plato, *The Republic*, 473d.
20 Plato, *The Republic*, 1102–3.

rule over us. Saints serve; they do not rule. But truth telling is not a saintly virtue; it is a moral virtue basic to any good and decent society. It is natural. We should expect our rulers to tell us the truth. Truth is not a lofty, noble goal to which rulers should aspire, but the ground floor that citizens should expect. As Plato saw first-hand, and history so often repeats, power without truth prepares the ground for tyranny.

Second, Plato helps us identify the tyrant. Tyranny, like evil in general, is seldom obvious, especially at first. If evil were obvious, it could easily be avoided. It is like the lie, a deceit appearing as something that is "good," a "delight" and even able to make one "wise" (see Genesis 3:6). What characterizes the tyrant most is a love of power and victory rather than truth. The tyrant disorders the soul of the city, putting victory and profit over everything, and being easily moved by flattery.[21] For Plato, if there is to be justice, truth must be held higher than wealth, honor, profit, or victory. The latter may have their place, but divided from the truth and pursued on their own, they generate vice. Vice cannot hold people together, at least not for long. Vicious bonds maintain their connectedness only through negative uses of force. Bonds of solidarity and friendship require the virtue of truth telling. They make for peace.

> **Tyrants wage war because they love power and victory rather than truth; peace requires truth telling.**

Third, if we lose philosophy, the love of wisdom, we will fail to learn from something that is more than we are. Only the present moment matters, only the "I" that "does." The past has no voice, making us more susceptible to the liar and demagogue. Lessons from the past, from history or tradition, will be dismissed by him as irrelevant. Along with the loss of philosophy and theology, the study of history is discarded. It cannot pass the test of quantitative assessments. Yet studying history matters; it is necessary for truth. Let me give an example.

---

21 Plato, *The Republic*, 1188–89.

In the summer of 2018, the then US attorney general, Jeff Sessions, implemented a zero-tolerance policy for immigrants and refugees illegally coming into the United States. As a deterrent, he enforced a law that was seldom enforced before, one that separated children from their parents and placed them in detention centers. He was not the first politician to use incarceration as a form of social control, but he accentuated it in novel and vicious ways. Many people from different political persuasions denounced the policy. Laura Bush penned a powerful letter in which she stated: "This zero-tolerance policy is cruel. It is immoral. And it breaks my heart."[22] It reminded her of another immoral moment in US history when Japanese people were interned in camps in World War II. Others likened the practice to that era of US history when the slavocrats made a point to remove slave children from their mothers at an early age.

Frederick Douglass (d. 1895), one of America's greatest philosophers and a former slave, wrote about this practice: "For what this separation is done, I do not know, unless it be to hinder the development of the child's affection towards its mother, and to blunt and destroy the natural affection of the mother for the child. This is the inevitable result."[23] Those words published in 1845 were sadly relevant again in the summer of 2018. The US government and ecclesial officials enforced similar family separation with the Native peoples, always purportedly for the children's own good. Others commented on the language the Trump administration and its supporters were using. The people seeking asylum were called invaders and an infestation. Critics noted how similar language has been used in the past in times that immediately preceded the committing of horrible acts against classes of people. General Michael Hayden and Senator Diane Feinstein invoked

---

22 "'It Is Immoral': Laura Bush Condemns Separation of Immigrant Children from Their Parents at the Border," *Dallas Morning News*, June 17, 2018, https://www.dallasnews.com/news/immigration/2018/06/17/immoral-laura-bush-condemns-separation-immigrant-children-parents-border.

23 "Narrative of the Life of Frederick Douglass," in *Douglass* (New York: Library of America, 1994), 16.

Nazi Germany. People are first reduced to the status of vermin, and then they can be treated as such. None of these persons, and the many others who made comparisons, were saying that the new policy was identical to slavery, the Japanese internment, or concentration camps. They were placing these actions in a history, cautioning those in power that they were treading some well-worn paths that never end well. The caution fell on deaf ears. Attorney General Sessions would hear none of it, defended his policy against all accusations, and stated: "Well, it's a real exaggeration. In Nazi Germany, they were keeping the Jews from leaving the country."[24] That obscene response demonstrated Sessions's complete lack of any historical sense, any awareness that his actions were nonidentically repeating historical narratives that he seemed to think did not matter. He could not hear, and he was, of course, wrong about Nazi Germany since the point of the camps was to exterminate Jews, not to keep them in the country.

Those defending the new practice of family separation used an argument similar to the one we saw Kellyanne Conway use in her discussion with Chuck Todd—the critics were being overly dramatic, exaggerating, falling prey to TDS (Trump Derangement Syndrome), and hyping the situation for reasons other than caring for the children. This, too, is a common practice of deceit—to marginalize dissenting voices by claiming that they are imbalanced, hysterical, possibly deranged. It is true that what occurred in the summer of 2018 is not the same as the practices in the slavocracy, the separation of Native American children, the Japanese internment camps, or the Nazi camps. Each of those differed significantly from it and from each other. The purpose of remembering these histories and raising them in protest against the new policy of family separation was to identify a genre, to place this activity in the context of similar, albeit different, activities in the past so that once the possibility of repeating the past is recognized, we might be more capable of putting an end to vicious repetitions. It is an

---

24 "Sessions Defends Zero Tolerance Immigration Policy," Fox News, June 18, 2018, online video clip, https://www.youtube.com/watch?v=Rxv2vxjW3i8.

attempt to get at the truth and do what can be done to ensure that the situation does not worsen. To remember is an essential moral act that requires humility and self-reflection. It requires us to interrogate ourselves, to ask about our sins "known and unknown." If someone refuses this posture and waits to speak until the situation has descended to the level of the demonic events perpetrated at Auschwitz, it will be too late. Cautionary tales must be told. To refuse to listen to them is to stand against truth telling.

Plato would have understood this, even if his solution is deeply troubling. On the one hand, he tells us that only when philosophers who love the truth coincide with politicians who hold power can we expect a just society. On the other, he tells us that a "noble lie" is necessary for the just society. To achieve harmony, he suggests that the following is necessary: "How, then, could we devise one of those useful falsehoods we were talking about a while ago, one noble falsehood that would, in the best case, persuade even the rulers, but if that's not possible, then the others in the city?"[25] The falsehood he tells is a religious story of creation. When God made the rulers, auxiliaries, and farmers and craftspersons, God made the first from gold, the second from silver, and the third from bronze. God then gave them a command: "So the first and most important command from the god to the rulers is that there is nothing that they must guard better or watch more carefully than the mixture of metals in the souls of the next generation." Then the god gave an oracle that stated, "The city will be ruined if it ever has an iron or a bronze guardian."[26] Religious myth sustains the lie. There are always "court chaplains" willing to use religion in service to political power for the sake of their own advantage. Philosopher-kings might begin to believe the lie themselves, especially once it has the backing of the court chaplains. If they do, power will be in service to the lie. Plato has explained what to avoid, but he has no way to avoid it without repeating it.

---

25 Plato, *The Republic*, 414c, 1050.
26 Plato, *The Republic*, 415 b–c.

Moses as Prophet-King

The question of Plato's *Republic* is, What kind of society do we need so that power will be in service to what is true and good? The question of justice quickly turns to the proper ordering of both the soul and the city, for harmony between them is necessary if there is to be justice. And just as reason must guide the passions and irrational appetites of the soul, so a just city will have rulers who subordinate force to truth. The theoretical contemplation of the soul and the practical knowledge required to craft a city will be united in the philosopher-king. The chances of a philosopher-king, however, are for Plato remote. The conditions necessary to have a just city are so unlikely that one way to read *The Republic* is as a realist who acknowledges that no one should expect just cities any more than one should expect philosopher-kings. Folks like Thrasymachus always come to power, and the wise like Socrates are their victims. Perhaps we should not look to politics or philosophy as the source for a truthful society. Perhaps we should look to religion. We now turn from philosophy to theology, from Plato's philosophy to Judaism and Christianity, exploring what they bring to the relationship between society and truth. This turn is hopeful because one should expect more from people of faith than one expects from those who seek to rule. Yet those hopes were dashed in 2016 because the emergence of Trumpism was possible in large part due to some Christian churches in the US.

Like many on the day of Trump's election, I was stunned, not because I had high hopes for US democratic processes or placed my trust in the Democratic Party, but in the end, I thought someone so indecent, so insulting of others, so obviously deceitful, would not persuade rural midwesterners or evangelical Christians. They were the people I grew up with, and I was stunned because I discovered that I no longer knew them. Some of them seemed to be more concerned with winning, the spectacle of crushing their enemies, and selfishness ("America First") than the values I thought that they instilled in me. Rowan Williams, archbishop of Canterbury, wrote an essay that expressed well the political and cultural failure Trump's election represented: "Trump's campaign succeeded in spite of his cast-iron demonstrations of his total indifference to truth (not to mention decency). . . . This election represents a divorce between the electoral process and the business of political decision making. It is the ersatz politics of mass theatre, in which what matters most is the declaration of victory."[27]

Mass democracy is an adversarial system that pits interest group against interest group.

In other words, our yearning for a true politics in which deliberating about what is good would matter gets sidetracked into a spectacle of power in which it seems as though we are being political, when we are, in truth, merely being entertained. For Williams, Trump's election is a clear demonstration of the failure of "mass democracy." Mass democracy is not actual democracy. It is an adversarial system that pits interest group against interest group, which is then managed by "fabulously well-resourced commercial and financial concerns." These well-resourced interests convinced some disenfranchised persons that their only option was Trump's political theatrics. The lack of any political alternative reflects one of the many failures in US politics. The Democratic Party has yet to demonstrate a substantive alternative to the theater of mass democracy. Williams suggests that "party politics" needs to be rethought in terms of a "local civic activism" that assumes people are capable of reasonable, political deliberation.

There is, however, one important piece missing in Williams's analysis, and that is the doctrine of white supremacy that contributed to Trump's election. Trump's campaign was implicitly and explicitly racist. Making a statement like that offends some sensibilities, and it is a good thing that it does. No one should want to be called a racist. So if we ascribe the moral label "racist" to

---

27 Rowan Williams, "Mass Democracy Has Failed—It's Time to Seek a Humane Alternative," *New Statesman America*, November 20, 2016, https://www.newstatesman.com/world/2016/11/mass-democracy-has-failed-its-time-seek-humane-alternative.

Trump and aspects of his campaign, those who resist it demonstrate a minimum moral commitment not to be racist, and that is preferable to those who celebrated Trump's victory as the triumph of their explicit white supremacy.

Four days after Trump's election, the Ku Klux Klan planned a celebratory march in North Carolina. It would be false to see this as an anomaly in US politics. The KKK had significant political power in both the southern and northern US for much of their history. I recall attending lunch with parishioners at a diner in rural North Carolina during my first appointment as a Methodist minister in the 1980s when the Klan marched outside the diner—and it was so normal that no one even looked up. It should not be forgotten that it was only in my lifetime that the US went from an explicit policy of segregation to an attempted integration, an attempt that left much unfinished business because white supremacy always finds new means for its purposes. As Michelle Alexander has persuasively demonstrated, Jim Crow did not disappear; it took on new forms.[28] Mass incarceration is another form of social control of black folk. Many of us were hopeful in 2015 that politicians might finally come together to address our much-needed prison reform. Its injustices are so obvious that even law-and-order conservatives were beginning to recognize it. The election of Trump and appointment of Jeff Sessions as attorney general put an end to any expectation that the gravest injustice perpetuated in the US would be addressed.

It is true, not an opinion, that white nationalists are ardent Trump supporters. The "alt-right," a term coined by the white nationalist Richard Spencer and his National Policy Institute, have a plan to so broaden what is normal in US politics that people begin to think the alt-right is normal. They use "freedom of speech" and the First Amendment to gain an audience for vile and dangerous rhetoric. They are smarter than the KKK because they have the same ideas but know that the term *KKK* scares people. After all, in the history of the US, the KKK is a terrorist organization that

---

28 Michelle Alexander, *The New Jim Crow: Mass Incarceration in the Age of Colorblindness* (New York: New Press, 2012), 11.

has done much more evil than ISIS has ever done or will do. The US will not become an Islamic caliphate, but it has been white nationalist with lynchings, Jim Crow, and slavery. The possibility of large swathes of the US being influenced by white nationalists is not out of the realm of possibility. The unwillingness of Trump and his administration to ask critical, reflexive questions as to why the KKK, the alt-right, and other white supremacists rejoiced at their election shows an utter lack of the virtue of humility and the need for historical memory.

I don't think it appropriate to call Trump a Nazi or a fascist. We are not repeating the 1930s, and speaking or acting as if we are does little good.[29] It misdescribes our moral and political moment. Trump is a racist, or, at a bare minimum, it should be noncontroversial to say he has made racist comments and committed racist acts. These examples should suffice (there are more): his statement about Judge Gonzalo Curiel, which Paul Ryan called "textbook racism"; the birther controversy; his proposed Muslim ban now implemented under another name with the imprimatur of the Supreme Court; the Charlottesville riots and his response; and the separation of brown children from their parents at the border. Calling Trump "racist" is not a subjective insult, an act of incivility; it is a moral description like calling Bill Clinton an adulterer.

It is important to get the right moral description if we want politics to be something more than pure will to power and winning. Politics can be, although it seldom is, the giving and receiving of practical reasons to arrive at what is good through the best account of truth that we can discover. I assume there is an objective morality. As a theologian, I assume it is in the mind of God and so God alone knows it, but God seeks to communicate it with

---

29 I don't mean to suggest that there are no similarities. The Holocaust historian Christopher R. Browning presents a brief but compelling account of the similarities and differences in his essay "The Suffocation of Democracy," *New York Review of Books*, October 25, 2018. He offers this evaluation: "Trump is not Hitler, and Trumpism is not Nazism, but regardless of how the Trump presidency concludes, this is a story unlikely to have a happy ending."

us and so we must seek after it, assuming that our politics at every level should aim for this goal (not the mind of God, but the good and truth communicated in creation), no matter how unrealizable. Theology should assist us in communicating truth; the failure of the churches in the US to communicate truth about our political situation requires that we return to our foundational sources in Scripture for the important practice of truth telling.

The Alexandrian Jew Philo (25 BC–50 AD) represents a good place to begin because he explicitly addressed Plato's question about the relationship between truth and power. But he did so, not through an imaginative construction of a just and true society but through the communication of such a society by God through Moses. In Philo's second book, *On the Life of Moses*, he states, "For it has been said, not without good reason, that cities only make progress in well-being if either kings are philosophers or philosophers are kings."[30] Power and wisdom should be united, but for Philo something more than a philosopher-king is necessary. There are three faculties beyond power and wisdom that are necessary for a just society—the ability (1) to give true and just laws, (2) to understand divine things, and (3) to render proper service through "perfect rites" that "perfect knowledge of the service of God." Moses is a leader preferable to any philosopher-king because he combines all these faculties in his person.

Moses rules a better city, a "Great City," as Philo calls it, not because he is a philosopher-king but because he is a king-priest-prophet. All these faculties matter, he states, so that "he may ask that he and those whom he rules may receive prevention of evil and participation in good from the gracious Being Who assents to prayers. For surely that Being will grant fulfilment to prayers, seeing that He is kindly by nature and deems worthy of His special favour those who give Him genuine service."[31] A crucial expression in that quote is "participation in good." For Philo—and here he is both similar to and different from Plato—what is good and

---

30 Philo, *On the Life of Moses*, *I*, in *The Works of Philo*, trans. C. D. Yonge (Peabody, MA: Hendrickson, 2006), 451.

31 Philo, *On the Life of Moses*, *I*, 453.

true is not simply what we make up for ourselves. In one sense, our post-truth politics assumes that the task of politics is not discovery but invention, and even beyond invention, mobilization, and manipulation. Invention first creates alternative facts. Politicians hire "communication" directors less for purposes of communicating and more for spinning the data in favor of the politician's interest. This spin is often what the term *politics* now signifies.

Think of the question that arises after a politician's actions, "How is it going to play politically?" That question does not ask, "What reasons are there for the politician's actions? Were they good or true?" Instead, it asks, "Will it motivate his base?" "Will it increase or decrease his favorability ratings?" But if this is what politics means, then it has already become untethered from truth telling and tethered to a cleverness to spin actions and statements through an imaginative construal that will mobilize votes or sentiments in the politician's favor. Politics is invention, not discovery. Such a politics does not require "participation in the good," which in Scripture is another term for "communication." To communicate is to receive and be taken up into something beyond one's self.

Philo tells us that a good and just society needs the prophet Moses because he knows that he is "but a mortal creature" who does not possess in his own strength the ability to rule. A true and good leader recognizes that he is a creature who stands before God in need. A truly righteous ruler, then, will need inspiration that goes beyond his own capacities; a leader needs the inspiration that prophecy provides. Moses fulfills Plato's lament for a philosopher-king because the laws Moses gives are "likenesses and copies of the patterns enshrined in the soul." The divine and mundane are united.

Of course, nonreligious persons are suspicious of such claims for prophecy, and for good reason. Prophecy among a certain sector of American Christianity has contributed to our post-truth society. Shortly after declaring that the US will move its embassy to Jerusalem and recognize that city as the capital of Israel, Donald Trump held one of his infamous rallies in Florida. One of the warm-up acts was Florida Republican state senator Doug Broxson, who made the following statement: "Now I don't know about you, but when I heard that Jerusalem, where the King of Kings, where our soon coming King is going to return back to Jerusalem, it is because President Trump declared Jerusalem to be the capital of Israel."[32] The apocalyptic and prophetic tradition among American Christian fundamentalists has led to such bizarre claims. Jesus's return depends upon Trump's policies, despite the harm that they might do. If this is what prophecy leads to, we are better off without "prophets." The role of the Christian church in the creation of our post-truth culture will be discussed more fully below, but suffice it for now to distinguish between a promethean prophetic spirit and the humble one Philo affirms. The promethean prophetic spirit understands prophecy as a weapon for a person or nation's own security and strength. It is a code to be cracked that favors the strong over the weak. It gives precise information that can be manipulated to force even God's hand. Senator Broxson conditions the Second Coming of Christ on the political actions of Donald Trump and the US government. Once we have the right people in power, then Jesus will return.

> It is not Moses's strength and power that conditions God's work; it is his weakness and humility.

Philo's humble prophetic spirit is the exact opposite of this. It is not Moses's strength and power that conditions God's work; it is his weakness and humility. Moses needs prophecy because he should not seek to create a city through his own might. As the Psalmist states, "God's delight is not in the strength of the horse, nor his pleasure in the speed of a runner, but the LORD takes pleasure in those who fear him, in those who hope in his steadfast love" (Psalms 147:10–11). Because Moses embodies a humble, prophetic spirit, he is also, writes Philo, "the best of all lawgivers in

---

32 Michael Stone, "Trump Rally Cheers Because Jerusalem Move Will Launch Armageddon," *Progressive Secular Humanist* (blog), December 9, 2017, http://www.patheos.com/blogs/progressivesecularhumanist/2017/12/trump-rally-cheers-jerusalem-move-will-launch-armageddon/.

all countries."[33] He receives God's law and promulgates it to others, including the rule necessary for the functioning of any good neighborhood, city, society, or nation—"Thou shalt not bear false witness." Yet Moses does not do this through force. He gives these laws under odd conditions, to people without land, military, or even a functioning government. All he has is communication of the divine word. We saw how Socrates responded to Polemarchus by suggesting persuasion would be better than force. Philo agrees and finds Moses to be a great ruler because he rules by persuasive speech rather than by the force of command.

Philo examines three kinds of rulers. The first are "legislators," who "command without exhortation." They are the worst form of leader because they rule without the use of persuasive, reasonable speech. Without it, the only thing that remains is force to implement law. In rejecting this first kind, Philo writes, "But Moses thinking that the former course, namely issuing orders without words of exhortation, as though to slaves instead of free men, savored of tyranny and despotism, as indeed it did." Words of exhortation are persuasive forms of speech—not spin, not manipulation, not incoherent rambling, but words grounded in truth. True leaders know and draw upon such words.

The second kind of leader Philo examines is preferable to the first; it is more like the philosopher-king whom Plato affirms. Such leaders exhort and subordinate power to wisdom and truth; they have something more than force behind their legislation. Yet, their exhortation is still an assertion of their own power because they first conceive a city in their imagination and then attach a "constitution . . . most agreeable and suitable to the form in which they had found it." Philo clearly has Plato's imaginative city from *The Republic* in mind. Although Philo is more favorable to this second kind of leader, it too was inadequate because "[Moses] considered that to begin his writings with the foundation of a man-made city was below the dignity of the laws." Law is not simply what we do; it is also something we receive. When it is divine communication, it creates the reality that we can discover.

---

33 Philo, *On the Life of Moses*, *I*, 457.

Philo thinks there is a third, better option found in the law given by God to Moses. This law is "greatness and beauty" that exceeds all "earthly walls." It constitutes "the story of the genesis of the 'Great City' holding that the laws were the most faithful picture of the world polity."[34] Moses as high priest, according to Philo, received the forms of the Great City when he went up the mountain and was given instructions on the "building and furnishing of the sanctuary."[35]

Receiving the "Great City" is central to the Jewish mission. Philo equates it with the construction of the Tabernacle. God gives to Moses "the immaterial forms" of the heavenly city, and in turn Moses uses them to establish the "material objects" of the Great City. Referring to the building of the tabernacle in Exodus 36–40, he states, "He saw with the soul's eye the immaterial forms of the material objects about to be made, and these forms had to be reproduced in copies perceived by the senses."[36] Philo sees in Moses the answer to Plato's question about the just society. Like Plato, he agrees that it cannot be had through mere command. The will to power is never an adequate basis for freedom or human flourishing. Unlike Plato, Philo disagrees that it can be had through human imagined constitutions.

> God's work is to create a people who dwell with God that they might make God's name holy by the way they live.

There is no human-centric politics of perfection. Human agency is not merely passive—the just society is received and that requires human action—but Moses has an insight that Plato never had. He sees the invisible things of God and brings them to the people in visible form. He does this by receiving sacred possessions and attending to them.

Philo, and Scripture's, emphasis on the Great City is all but forgotten in much of contemporary Christianity, but neither Christianity nor Judaism makes sense without a mission to serve

---

34 Philo, *On the Life of Moses*, *I*, 473–75.
35 Philo, *On the Life of Moses*, *I*, 485.
36 Philo, *On the Life of Moses*, *I*, 541.

the Great City. Too often contemporary Christianity is reduced to "personal" salvation, as if what God is doing in the world is saving individuals from creation for an eternal realm unrelated to everyday, temporal life. This false, modern Christianity is waiting for Jesus to come back to Jerusalem, kill all the enemies of Christianity, and rapture the real Christians away from this world as it is engulfed in flames. It is a heretical view of Christianity invented in modernity that will not endure because Scripture offers little to no support for it. This faulty view of salvation has contributed to the selfishness present in much of contemporary Christianity as well.

Perhaps this is why US Christians can think their faith compatible with "America First," an unbiblical and self-centered program that could garner only divine wrath. God's work is not to save individuals but to create a people who will dwell with God and God with them that they might make God's name holy by the way in which they live. This way of life is particular; it is first given to the Jews. It is also universal; it is intended for all. Essential to the way of life that unites heaven and earth is that it observes the ninth commandment, "Thou shalt not lie" or "You shall not bear false witness against your neighbor" (Exodus 20:16). This commandment, like the other nine in the Ten Commandments, or the other 612 "mitzvot," are charitable deeds one performs fulfilling the heart of the commandments—love God and neighbor. We fulfill both by telling the truth to each other before God. It is why we pray, "To You all hearts are open, all desires known, and no secrets are hidden." We need not live as people of truth in the presence of each other, but we cannot but live as such before God. Torah is, as many biblical commentators have suggested, not merely laws to be observed by individuals but a social program that prepares us to live with God.

> The lie unavoidably perpetuates violence and then seeks to justify it.

Receiving the Great City is the mission God gives to Abraham and Sarah as the means to repair the wounds humanity inflicts on creation. Those wounds began with the lie, as we saw above, when our mother Eve became susceptible to it. After the lie came violence. Cain kills his brother Abel. One must not forget that the lie and violence are always related. One way to identify the lie is to see the violence it unavoidably perpetuates and then justifies. Violence begets violence, and then a cycle of revenge emerges. Lamech slays someone for wounding him, and God sees that the "earth is filled with violence" because of human creatures (Genesis 6:13). God redeems it first by saving Noah and his family through the waters of purification, but all is still not well. Human creatures decide to make their own city, "to make a name for themselves." Here is a key source to the rejection of the "Great City." We seek to build our own city, our own towers, with our name emblazoned on them. A tower extended to the heavens with our name emblazoned upon it is a sign of human depravity. Why did this never occur to the court chaplains who so quickly endorsed Trump? Human creatures seek a strong and secure city with a tower that will rival the heavenly city (Genesis 11:4). God's merciful act is to prevent that city by scattering them into nations and languages.

What God scatters, God then begins to collect and reunite. But it cannot be done in just any way. It cannot be done through the force of command, or God will simply repeat the cycle of sin, deceit, and violence that led us to the place where we desire a rival tower with our name hoisted upon it. God collects and unites through persuasive rhetoric, through the Word. God communicates with Abraham and Sarah and gives them a mission by which they will be a blessing to all. God says: "I will make of you a great nation, and I will bless you, and make your name great, so that you will be a blessing. I will bless those who bless you, and the one who curses you I will curse; and in you all the families of the earth shall bless themselves" (Genesis 12:2–3). Their mission is not to be like the nations for the sake of the nations. They are not to be like the nations because their society is not built and defended by their own strength and imagination or by the lie. It comes to them as a gift, the gift of God's name, which is truth. It comes to them through the Torah, and right worship.

After God gives a mission to Abraham and Sarah and before the Torah is given to Moses, God gives Israel God's name. God's name is "I AM." It is from this name that the Holy Name YHWH arises. The name is so holy that it can only be said on specific occasions, such as the Day of Atonement in the Holy of Holies. The high priest enters sacred space and speaks God's name. The result is that heaven and earth can continue to dwell together. There is a long tradition of correlating God's name with truth; this should be unsurprising. For ancient philosophers, truth depends on being. As we have already noted, and will note again, Aristotle defines truth as saying of what is that it is and of what is not that it is not. God's name, "I AM," is the fullness of being, and thus another name for God throughout Christian tradition is "the First Truth." The Roman Catholic Catechism teaches the importance of God as truth for obeying the commandment not to take God's name in vain. To speak the truth is to honor God's name. To lie is to dishonor it. It relates this commandment to every human utterance, bringing together the second commandment, "Do not take God's name in vain," with the eighth commandment, "You shall not bear false witness against your neighbor," and states: "Rejection of false oaths is a duty toward God. As Creator and Lord, God is the norm of all truth. Human speech is either in accord with or in opposition to God who is Truth itself. When it is truthful and legitimate, an oath highlights the relationship of human speech with God's truth. A false oath calls on God to be a witness to a lie."[37] Each act of speech cannot but bear on a relationship to God because language is one of God's created gifts and how it is used reflects how we treat God's good creatures.

> To speak the truth honors God.

Language allows us to communicate, to present ourselves to each other as God presents God's self to us. It is an awesome responsibility and brings with it a prima facie duty to speak the truth. It is a prima facie duty because there are moments when speaking the truth or keeping a promise might not be owed to someone. As the *Catechism* notes, there is a qualification—"when

---

37 *Catechism of the Catholic Church*, paragraph 2151, http://www.vatican
.va/archive/ccc_css/archive/catechism/p3s2c1a2.htm.

it is truthful and legitimate." There are famous cases in which phi-losophers and theologians have suggested that a *bare* truth tell-ing would not be morally warranted. For instance, suppose you borrowed a weapon from someone and promised to return it to him. He gets intoxicated and in an irrational fit of rage decides to kill a neighbor. He comes and asks you to return the weapon as you promised. Knowing the context within which he plans to use it, most ethicists would suggest that for the sake of your neighbor you are not under obligation to keep the promise at that moment. It would not be legitimate. This case is relatively easy, how-ever, because there is an important distinction between break-ing a promise and lying. The conditions under which promises are made and kept change. Those changes affect the intention behind one's vows. A more difficult case would be when security officers are pursuing an unjust law. Perhaps they are slave patrols looking for escaped slaves, Nazis looking for Jews, or ICE looking to separate migrant children from their parents in order to deter refugees seeking asylum. In each of these cases, you are hiding the persons they seek to detain and harm. What does truth telling require in these contexts? If truth serves injustice, do you owe the truth to the person who seeks to use it for a nefarious purpose? Many reasonable people would say no in these exceptional cases because the virtue of truth telling conflicts with that of justice, and virtues cannot and should not conflict. However, they are excep-tional cases, and exceptional cases often prove the rule showing what it means to obey the commandment "Do not lie."[38]

Others suggest that not lying is always an obligation. The vir-tue of truth telling permits equivocation, as Joan of Arc did when

---

38 The question these exceptional circumstances raise should not lead us into a simple either-or: either tell the truth and commit injustice or lie and preserve justice. As a virtue, truth telling requires social contexts that privilege truth and preserving justice. An example where this hap-pened is in the mountain village of Le Chambon, where a Hugenot com-munity structured their life together so that they could hide Jews and not lie to the police. (See Philip Haillie's *Lest Innocent Blood Be Shed* [New York: HarperPerennial, 1994].)

she put a cross at the end of her letters letting her readers know that she intended the opposite of what she wrote, confusing spies who might get them.[39] Telling lies is a serious moral matter because, as we have seen, the lie lives beyond itself. Practical wisdom is necessary to discern how not to lie in exceptionally difficult cases.

> **Truth telling is a basic and necessary good; society cannot exist without it.**

Truth telling is a basic and necessary good. Society cannot exist without it, and how we use language is always related to how we use God's name. Not to use God's name in vain does not mean not to utter profanity but, rather, not to use God's name for empty things. To speak a lie is to use God's name for empty things. To spin the truth for the sake of personal advantage is to use God's name for empty things. To invoke God's name for purposes alien to God's nature and will is the height of using God's name in vain. Among the greatest failures of the Christian church that contributes to our post-truth culture are the multiple violations of the second commandment that have defined the Christian life in these United States: Christian nationalism, American exceptionalism, prosperity Christianity, white supremacy are all vain uses of God's name.

Not only does God give Moses God's name and the Torah, God also provides explicit direction for a tabernacle within which the Torah will be placed, and God's holy name uttered. It is where God dwells on earth, the place where heaven and earth meet. It is composed of three parts: an outer courtyard, a holy place, and the holy of holies. The ark of the covenant is placed in the holy of holies. The glory of God resides in this ark, and the covenant made with Israel is placed in it (Exodus 25:10–16). A mercy seat of pure gold is placed on top of the ark, with two gold cherubim surrounding it. God meets God's people at this place: "There I will meet with you, and from above the mercy seat, from between the two cherubim that are on the ark of the covenant, I will deliver

---

39 See Peter Geach, *The Virtues* (Cambridge: Cambridge University Press, 1977), 120–21.

to you all my commands for the Israelites" (Exodus 25:22). Once the tabernacle was finished, Exodus teaches that God visited it: "Then the cloud covered the tent of meeting, and the glory of the LORD filled the tabernacle. Moses was not able to enter the tent of meeting because the cloud settled upon it, and the glory of the LORD filled the tabernacle. Whenever the cloud was taken up from the tabernacle, the Israelites would set out on each stage of their journey; but if the cloud was not taken up, then they did not set out until the day that it was taken up" (Exodus 40:34–37).

As we saw above, Philo interpreted the tabernacle as the origins of the Great City that God is crafting and the Torah as the divine communication Moses was given for this city. Christianity is unintelligible apart from this Jewish expectation of the Great City. It is the hoped-for city that comes to us in the priest-king Jesus. In fact, John 1 draws upon the imagery in Exodus 40 to present who Jesus is. Forgetting truth is forgetting Jesus. "Do this in remembrance of me" cannot coexist with a will to forget the past. One or the other must be abandoned.

Jesus as Priest-King

Plato posed a question about the relationship between a just society and truth. If justice is nothing but the advantage of the stronger, then truth is at best a façade that hides what really makes society what it is—power and advantage. Plato imagines an alternative just society, but his construction still bases the harmony of society on a "noble lie." Philo answers Plato's question with divine communication. Moses does not imagine a just society and then implement it; he receives the beginning of a "great City" from God in which God and creatures dwell together in harmony. Central to this city is truth telling, including using God's name properly and not bearing false witness.

The Gospel of John depicts Jesus as the site of the Great City. John 1:14 states, "The Word became flesh and dwelt among us." As many biblical scholars and theologians have pointed out, the term for "dwelt" here is the same as that for the "tabernacle" in the Greek translation of Exodus. A good translation would be: "The Word became flesh and tabernacled among us." The term matters for the following reasons. First because of the importance of the Great City for the Jewish and Christian mission. The mission of Abraham and Sarah was to serve the nations by not being like the nations. Moses inherited that mission, and Yahweh constructs a site where divine glory and human creatures live as one. The "glory of God" fills the tabernacle, making it holy. Second, Jesus is now identified with both the tabernacle and the glory of God. John 1:14 continues, "The Word became flesh and tabernacled among us, full of grace and truth, and we have beheld his glory, glory as of the only Son from the Father." He is the manifestation of divine glory. Third, the glory of God Jesus reveals is inextricably linked with truth. Jesus is "full of grace *and truth*."

Truth is a central theme running throughout John's Gospel because God's glory cannot be beheld without also beholding truth. Jesus is the "true light" that enlightens everyone (1:9). As Moses gives the law, so Jesus gives grace and truth (1:17). Those who "do what is true" will be attracted to the light (3:21). God is identified with truth (3:33) and is to be worshipped "in spirit and truth" (4:24). John the Baptist bears witness to the truth, who is Jesus (5:33). The Pharisees challenge the truth of Jesus's testimony, and Jesus responds that his testimony is true because the one who sent him is true, once again identifying God with truth. Jesus tells those who follow him that if they would be his disciples, they will know the truth, "and the truth will make you free" (8:32). God as truth is contrasted with the devil, who is the "father of lies" (8:44). Jesus tells his disciples that he must depart from them, but they need not worry because he will prepare a place for them, and Thomas responds in fear that they do not know the way. Jesus responds, "I am the way, and the truth, and the life" (14:6) and promises to give them the "spirit of truth" (14:17). Jesus prays for his disciples that God will "sanctify them in truth," and that he and they would be "consecrated in truth" (17:17–19). Jesus is full of grace and truth because he is the manifestation of the promised site in which God and creatures dwell together in unity, but the "world" to which Christians should not be conformed has a different politics altogether—a politics indifferent to truth.

The famous scene between Jesus and Pilate is a contest between two forms of life. Until this point in the Gospel of John, the contest is primarily between Jesus and the Pharisees about bearing true witness. Neither of them denies the centrality of truth. In one sense, it would be appropriate to read the first seventeen chapters of John as an extended commentary on the eighth commandment. Those chapters address what it is to bear true testimony. When Pilate enters the praetorium and calls Jesus to him, the terms of the contest change. It no longer concerns how to embody the commandment to bear true testimony; it now concerns whether truth matters at all.

Pilate first asks Jesus a political question, "Are you the King of the Jews?" As we know from the rest of the story, it is this charge that gets Jesus crucified. It is placed over his head on the cross as the sentence that warrants his death. Jesus responds to Pilate's question by asking a bold question—Is he asking this of his own accord or under the influence of others? Here stands Pilate who holds the power to sentence Jesus, and any other Jew, to death; and Jesus questions if he is truly in charge, as he thinks he is. Pilate responds in scorn that he is not a Jew, and it is Jesus's own nation that has handed him over. Jesus responds by saying that his kingdom is not of this world, affirming that he is a king. Jesus is not claiming that his kingship is otherworldly in the sense that it is located somewhere other than creation; in John's Gospel, "world" most often signifies creation gone awry. Jesus's response to Pilate's reiteration of his original question, "So you are a king?," reveals how his politics is present. It is standing before Pilate: "You say that I am a king. For this I was born, and for this I have come into the world, to bear witness to the truth. Everyone who is of the truth hears my voice." Pilate's response, "What is truth?," discloses his worldly politics (John 18:33–38). Truth is not something that can be present, generating politics. Leadership is not about truth, but power. Pilate stands with Thrasymachus. He shows his power by ruling that Jesus must be crucified because Caesar will not allow rival kings (19:12–16). Pilate considers himself the one in charge, the one who decides Jesus's fate, but Jesus's question should be kept in mind—Are Pilate's actions his own, or are his vicious actions serving a truth that he does not know how to see? In mocking Jesus like a king and lifting him up on the cross, Pilate has enthroned Jesus for all to see, but the result was not the anticipated obedience to death and power that Roman rule expected, but life. For Jesus's way, the way of the cross, is the truth that leads to life, resurrection life. Every time the church gathers for worship, it re-presents Jesus's enthronement, signifying that he has established a Great City that is here even though it is not of this world.

Jesus's kingship is another answer to Plato's question, How might we live in a just city whose ruler orders our common life toward truth? We see this not only in John's Gospel but also in the letter to the Hebrews. The book of Hebrews has no explicit response to Plato as Philo did, but it may have been influenced by Philo. When read as a response, explicit or implicit, to Philo's response to Plato's quest for a philosopher-king, several aspects of Hebrews gain intelligibility. First, it makes sense as to why Jesus is not depicted as prophet but contrasted with prophecy. Moses already has that role; Jesus's role differs. Second, it shows why the two main roles Jesus fulfills are those of king and priest, and why those roles have now become intertwined. Third, it lets us know why it matters that Jesus rules a city/temple not made by mortal hands. Fourth, it explains why so many admonitions are strewn throughout the sermon, and the sermon itself is presented as a "word of exhortation." It also provides insight for what otherwise appears to be random bits of information scattered here and there such as the importance of discerning good from evil, and mundane regulations.

Hebrews begins by contrasting God's speaking in the Son to what was spoken to the fathers in the prophets. According to Philo, Moses needed prophecy because he was a "mortal creature," and reason could not attain "countless things" both "human and divine" that are "wrapped in obscurity" without divine inspiration. Prophecy provided what was lacking.[40] A "son," however, according to Hebrews, has less need of prophecy, especially when he is the "exact imprint of God's very being" (1:3). Although Hebrews

---

40 Philo, *On the Life of Moses*, I, 453.

places prophetic words in Jesus's mouth (10:5b–7), the focus is not on Jesus as prophet; it is on his roles as king and priest. Those roles are established in the first two chapters, before Jesus as Son is found "worthy of more glory" than Moses the servant in chapter 3. If Moses answers Plato's question because he is, for Philo, a prophet, Jesus answers it because he is, for Hebrews, Son.

Hebrews depicts the Son straightaway as "king." The first verse begins with his royal enthronement (1:3) and those that follow speak of his "throne" (1:9). He is then "crowned" (2:7), and all things are placed in subjection to him (2:8). But his is an odd kingship, for it is won by his activity as a "faithful and merciful high priest in service to God" (2:17). It is not power but faith and mercy that fit him for rule. His priesthood is as odd as his kingship. Jesus is not from the tribe of the Levites, the tribe from which priests come. His priesthood comes from Melchizedek, himself both priest and king, but it exceeds that of Melchizedek by Jesus's once-and-for-all sacrifice in which he is both priest and victim. It is offered not in the temporal temple made by hands, but in the eternal temple, God's dwelling place, where the king-priest reigns.

Hebrews 5 tells us that as high priest Jesus was "made perfect" and that he offers a sacrifice that also perfects (5:9). He fulfills the role of offering perfect rites that perfect others that Philo attributed to Moses. Philo claimed these divine things are necessary for the "prevention of evil" and "participation in good." Hebrews concludes the discussion of Jesus's perfect offering on a similar note, chiding his hearers that they do not yet live on "solid food," which is "for the mature [or perfect], for those whose faculties have been trained by practice to distinguish good from evil" (5:14). The discernment between good and evil lacks context to render it intelligible. Why did the author move from Jesus's perfect offering to his hearers' discrimination of good from evil? It seems a non sequitur. But if he assumed his hearers knew something of Philo's argument, it makes more sense. Jesus as priest-king is fashioning the truly just city. Such a city does what all good cities do, prevent evil and encourage good. This discernment is what its citizens, Hebrews' listeners, should have embodied and exercised, but they are not yet able to do so. The book of Hebrews is the author's attempt to form them into such a proper citizenship through persuasive discourse.

Jesus as priest-king is Ruler not of a city crafted by human architects, but of a city God is preparing for them. As in Philo, the image of the city and that of the temple merge. Jesus is high priest of the "perfect tent (not made with hands . . .)." It is God's city, the city of faithful rest, for which all the faithful waited: "For he [Abraham] looked forward to the city that has foundations, whose architect and builder is God" (11:10). The faithful were unwilling to settle for anything less:

> They confessed that they were strangers and foreigners on the earth, for people who speak in this way make it clear that they are seeking a homeland. If they had been thinking of the land that they had left behind, they would have had opportunity to return. But as it is, they desire a better country, that is a heavenly one. Therefore God is not ashamed to be called their God; indeed, he has prepared a city for them. (11:13b–16)

That same city has been prepared for those who listen to the message from Hebrews if they "hold fast the confession" that they received. "For here we have no lasting city, but we are looking for the city that is to come" (13:14). One of the church's greatest failures in the US has been its willingness to settle for something less, for power over truth, for religious nationalism rather than patiently waiting for the Great City and acting even now as citizens of it.

Strewn throughout Hebrews are admonitions, words of exhortation, to hold firm the "confidence," the "substance," and the "confession" (3:6, 14; 4:14; 10:23). This confidence and confession are confusing. Hebrews provides no creed that constitutes the confession. We are told in 11:13, however, that those who "died in faith without having received the promises . . . confessed that they were strangers and foreigners on the earth." The confession appears to have both a negative and positive dimension. The negative dimension is that they have no just city now, no place they can call home. The positive dimension is that they do have an already established city, one not built by human hands and over which Jesus already rules. He does not rule it by force but is nonetheless administering it. He does so, much as the author of Hebrews himself, by admonition and exhortation. Hebrews' listeners are not promised that they will triumph over their oppressors; they are not promised wealth. They are promised that God will shake the earth and that only what is solid will stand. Hebrews concludes chapter 12 with this important admonition: "Therefore, since we are receiving a kingdom that cannot be shaken, let us give thanks, by which we offer to God an acceptable worship with reverence and awe; for indeed our God is a consuming fire" (12:28–29). The sermon is a "word of exhortation." For Philo, this kind of word was what made Moses a better ruler than Plato's philosopher-king. What we see in Hebrews is not so much a city constructed in speech, as we saw with Plato's *Republic*, as the actual performance of truthful discourse: exhortation to confident confession in a city we do not yet see, but one that has been established by the priest-king.

If it makes sense to read Hebrews responding to Philo responding to Plato, then Hebrews can be viewed as a treatise on the just and true society. Jesus subordinates political rule to perfection through his obedient suffering. He builds a city not made by human hands, but this does not make it only otherworldly or supernatural. The concluding mundane regulations that could seem anticlimactic or out of place given the grand claims the sermon makes—"Let mutual love continue. Do not neglect to show hospitality to strangers. Remember those who are in prison. Let marriage be held in honor by all. Keep your lives free from the love of money"—make perfect sense. Far from inviting us to flee from the world, to abandon or hate it, Hebrews calls for us to strengthen what cannot be shaken. Once the anxiety of establishing political rule has been assuaged because that rule has already been established, it frees us from the tyranny of waiting for a philosopher-king. The wait was proper. Plato was correct. Power must be subordinated to truth. Jesus is the truth that is at the same time divine power, manifest in the cross and resurrection.

Hebrews is not religious rather than political, or eternal rather than temporal; it is, like Plato's soul and city, both at the same time. True cites are not founded upon the advantage of the stronger, even when it looks otherwise. Politics is a matter of patience and truth telling, of enduring ordinary life consistent with the Ruler who has already triumphed. It requires gathering Sunday after Sunday for his kingly enthronement via Word and Sacrament and learning to view society through his peculiar rule. The eternal and temporal merge. Our politics should not be founded upon force and coercion but upon admonition and persuasion. We can take the time to do so because of the confidence that there is a city already established that promises rest.

Power must be subordinate to truth.

Conclusion

We live in a post-truth culture. Trump makes that obvious, but such a culture was long in the making. He intensified it, brought it to some unsavory conclusions, and made us all participants in it. Alternative facts, "truth isn't truth," demagogic speeches, hurling insults, confusion, deflection, gaslighting, racial dog whistling have become our new normal. No one yet knows where it will lead or how to confront it. Responding in kind does not work because someone who prevaricates without purpose can descend to indecent depths to which few are willing or able to descend. The previous examples of Plato, Philo, and Jesus are attempts to set our minds on a more noble trajectory. The question is, Who is the "we"? Who is the audience that can hear and hold fast to these examples? Who recognizes the problem Plato identified, a problem manifest once again before our eyes?

Two different groups have been addressed in this first chapter. One is the US nation-state. The other is the Christian church. Expectations for each differ. Throughout this work, and especially in the final chapter, I will attempt to set forth our roles as citizens in both the nation-state and the church. Those roles differ. We do not expect the nation-state to perfect us. It does not have the means to do so. It is not the Great City for which we wait. It is no city set on the hill, but this should not mislead us into accepting tyranny and confusion or into becoming susceptible to the lie.

Truth telling is a basic virtue available to all simply on the basis of being creatures. It is an obligation to hold everyone accountable to it. More should be expected from the church. It should not be in service to an earthly society making us more susceptible to the lie.

> **Truth telling is available to all. It carries an obligation to hold everyone accountable to it, especially the church, which should not be in service to an earthly society, thereby making us more susceptible to the lie.**

Perhaps we should not expect too much from our earthly societies. I agree with those who remind us that we should not expect those who rule over us to be saints. The two ways of life—pursuit of power and pursuit of holiness—often conflict. Nonetheless, truth telling is a basic, not a saintly, pursuit. We should expect it from earthly societies if we want them to contribute to human flourishing. If we have become complacent about such expectations, it is a sign that we too have become comfortable with the lie. We may never get a philosopher-king, but we should unceasingly seek to hold our leaders accountable to truth for the sake of a good society. No one—journalists, clergy, teachers, artists, welders, every citizen and neighbor—has an excuse for being taken in by the lie and refusing to tell the truth. Truth telling is a task for all, and if we lose it, we will get the leadership we deserve.

More should be expected from the church than mere truth telling, but certainly nothing less. To those within the church, Abraham and Sarah, Moses, and Jesus are reminders that the service the church renders to the world is first to be a community of truth telling in its own life and second to witness to the truth both by the way it conducts its life before others and what it expects of others. Those who are without the church, members of other religions, secular persons, should hold us accountable to the virtue of truth telling. As noted above, our relation to God as "the First Truth" is directly related to a truthful use of language. The fact that Christians in the US so readily abandoned this commitment for the sake of power is reason to question if Christianity is true, or at least, if the dominant view of Christianity in the US is true.

What I find deeply disturbing about the US church's complicity in Trumpism is its spiritual blindness; it either has not received or does not exercise the gift of discernment. It has the witness of Scripture, but it sides with secular power. The Trump administration's brazen prevarications are the logical outcome of secular modernity. Iris Murdoch, a committed atheist, has better discernment than the court chaplains who have misled so many in the present generation. She explained the ideal person secular modernity generates. First, she argued, the moral philosopher Kant had unintentionally "abolished God and made man God in His stead." We live in the "age of the Kantian man." What characterizes this age is that the will is the "creator of value." Whatever is considered to be true, whatever is considered to be good, is nothing but the assertion of the will, the will to power. Truth is what I say is true in the moment even if I contradict it in the next one. She went on to argue that it is not that far from Kant to Nietzsche. Yet it was Milton who identified this type of man much earlier: "His proper name is Lucifer."[41] We have lost any sensibility for the demonic, and what is most ironic is that those who profess to still have that sensibility have proven themselves least equipped to discern it.

> Truth is basic to a just society that seeks to avoid tyranny.

Why should truth matter? Truth is not only for the religious. It is basic to a just society that seeks to avoid tyranny. Societies must use power. Chapter 3 will offer a crash course on political philosophy that tries to offer some bearing on the relations among the state, nations, civil society, the church, and uses of power, force, coercion, and violence. Given the exclusive use of the means of violence handed over to the state, what offers the brakes to its

---

41   Iris Murdoch, "Sovereignty of Good over Other Concepts," in *Virtue Ethics,* ed. Roger Crisp and Michael Slote (Oxford: Oxford University Press, 1997), 101.

exercise of power? Truth is one such brake. Losing it makes us more susceptible to unaccountable uses of power, coercion, and violence. For that reason, everyone should have a stake in telling the truth. Truth is also a theological practice and concept. God is the First Truth. It is in God's image that we are created. As creatures, we cannot but participate in truth. It is unavoidable. However, we can participate in it poorly, using it not for good purposes but for wickedness. We learn the vice of lying. To lie, to bear false witness, is to use God's name in vain even when the name "God" is not invoked. To tell the truth, about one's self, one's nation, one's church, is to be set free. It is to stand with Moses and Jesus. To normalize the lie is to turn our backs on them and find our exemplars in Thrasymachus, Pilate, and Nietzsche. Truth matters because it says something about the company we keep.

WILL POWER FREE YOU?

The previous chapter raised Plato's question about the relationship between truth and power and looked to Moses and Jesus for answers to that question. It tried to make a case that truth matters if we want to stand in their company for they stand in the company of God. It was necessary to begin with truth because it is more basic to our existence and necessary for our common life than what is false, than the lie. This chapter examines the lie, examining its power and hold over us. It asks whether Jesus spoke the truth in saying that truth will set us free. There is another possibility, one that looks without blinking into the hard reality of power and states that it, rather than truth, is the basis for freedom. Thucydides, Thrasymachus, Pilate, and Nietzsche reflect that tradition. It rejects the claim that truth frees us and thus opposes Plato, Abraham and Sarah, Moses, Philo, and Jesus. They are contending traditions. No one can stand in both. The latter makes the bold claim that the truth will set you free. Truth is a condition for freedom. If there is no truth, there is no freedom. The former laughs at such nonsense. Truth is a "worn-out metaphor" that does not work. The proper responses to claims for truth are: What is a fact? What is truth? We have alternative facts. Truth isn't truth. Truth is nothing but virtue signaling. Truth, like justice, is a mask for power.

As I noted in the previous chapter, "The truth will set you free" is the motto of the university where I work. Like many universities, its motto, which was selected in 1912, reflects its Christian legacy. These words remain present in the university, marking significant moments and monuments of the university's life and architecture. Nearly one hundred years after they were first chosen, the university's president referred to them in his 2011 opening convocation address. The motto, he stated, "takes the primary goal of educational pursuits (Truth) and makes it the antecedent of one of the major drives within the human heart: Freedom."[1] The motto, like the biblical passage on which it is based, assumes that if you want to be free, truth is one of its conditions. The primary purpose of the university is to pursue truth, and in so doing it contributes to freedom. Is that assumption warranted? Will the truth set us free? We already saw how Washington State University's administration was silent when the football coach questioned the virtue of truth telling. They are not alone among universities. Such silence stands not with the assumption that truth sets us free; it stands with Thrasymachus—advantage, power, and injustice are as much the condition for freedom as truth or goodness. It stands with Pilate. If there is any truth, we cannot know it. Closer to our time, it stands with Nietzsche's diagnosis of the modern era—truth, like all higher values, has disvalued itself. It no longer matters.

Truth or power— which brings freedom?

This chapter's purpose is to illumine nihilism, which is generally understood as the rejection of all religious and moral principles. It also often holds the belief that life is meaningless. Countless editorials, politicians, and others have referred to the rise of Trump as the consequence of nihilism. We are told that "we will all pay

---

1   Gerald R. Turner, "SMU Opening Convocation," 2011, https://www.smu .edu/EnrollmentServices/Registrar/AcademicCeremonies/AboutUs/ History/Motto.

a price for Trump's nihilism,"[2] that Trump's election shows that conservatism ends in nihilism,[3] that the very "idea of Trump" is a "sort of nihilism,"[4] and that with Trump, "America has accelerated its most insidious tendency: nihilism";[5] even a retiring Republican congressman has referred to the "Trump era" as "nihilism."[6] Each of these persons, and many more could be included, identify Trumpism with nihilism. For some, Trump represents an exception to a previous era that was not nihilistic. For others, he represents a logical outgrowth of Western tendencies, and especially US culture, that have the seeds of nihilism present in them. Those seeds are often found in the marketplace. It is no surprise that the desire to have a businessman in the White House leads to accusations of nihilism.

Nihilism and the Loss of Truth

The diagnosis of Western society as nihilistic has been around for two hundred years. Nihilism has been associated with the dominance of market society over most aspects of life, a society known

---

2 Eugene Robinson, "We Will All Pay a Price for Trump's Nihilism," *Washington Post,* November 27, 2017, https://www.washingtonpost.com /opinions/we-will-all-pay-a-price-for-trumps-nihilism/2017/11/27 /2be5d924-d3b1-11e7-95bf-df7c19270879_story.html?utm_term =.123ffe6276b7.

3 Mike Lofgren, "Will Conservatism End in Nihilism?," *Washington Monthly,* January 3, 2018, https://washingtonmonthly.com/2018/01/03/ will-conservatism-end-in-nihilism/.

4 Victor Davis Hanson, "Trump: Something New under the Sun," *National Review,* May 3, 2016, https://www.nationalreview.com/2016/05/donald -trump-his-supporters/.

5 Pankaj Mishra, "America, From Exceptionalism to Nihilism," *New York,* April 28, 2017, https://www.nytimes.com/2017/04/28/opinion/america -from-exceptionalism-to-nihilism.html.

6 Andrew Desiderio, "Retiring GOP Congressman: Trump-Era 'Nihilism' Bad for America," *Daily Beast,* September 18, 2017, https://www.the dailybeast.com/retiring-gop-congressman-trump-era-nihilism-bad-for -america.

for its commitment to value or utility over truth. Yet we should be careful about subscribing too quickly either to a narrative of decline or one of inevitable progress. "Truth" may be more difficult to affirm in 2018 than it was in 1912, but not all the reasons why are negative. We have positive reasons to be cautious about too-quick references to truth. We look back at 1912 and see the carnage that was present, or soon would be present, and affirmations that the truth will set us free did little to call them into question. As we will see in chapter 3, the power of the Ku Klux Klan was rejuvenated shortly after 1912. Many elected politicians, and even a Supreme Court justice, publicly self-identified as Klansmen. Jim Crow, the repression of women, two world wars culminating in indiscriminate warfare and a massive refugee crisis, anti-Semitism leading to the Holocaust—these and other injustices should prevent us from any wrongheaded sentimental longing for the "good old days" or the assumption that somehow we had a truthful society then but lost it at a later point in time and must return to it. The Klan resurfaced as people who claimed to be telling the truth, as did men who made laws that kept women in their place. Neither blacks nor women were given the power white men had to question what they assumed was truth.

Truth telling may be more difficult in 2018 than it was in 1912 because we have rightly become chastened by easy appeals to truth that overlook the power relations that they hid. This is a positive gain for society. When anyone claims that they want to make America great again, the question must be asked, What do they think has been lost and why should it return? It must be remembered that the "good old days" were not good for everyone. Change, revision, reform, even revolution can be liberating—but not always. Change can bring decline rather than progress.

Easy appeals to truth can overlook the power relations they hide.

A negative reason that truth telling is more difficult is the flip side of the previously mentioned positive gain. We live in an age encumbered with nihilism that has become wary of appeals to truth, as it has become wary of anything older than what has just occurred. The modern era, and the economics internal to it, views change almost always as preferable to what came before. The word *change* can be, and has been, a political slogan by itself, even though it is meaningless. Change for change's sake, with no end in sight, with no purpose that could provide rest for the unceasing change, has become the cultural default. There is no seventh day, no honoring the Sabbath. There is only 24/7, a recurring cyclical change with no purpose. One of the influential economists of the twentieth century, Joseph Schumpeter (1883–1950), identified the dynamic behind capitalism as this kind of change, calling it "creative destruction." It generates wealth by destroying old ways of doing things in favor of new ones. The bicycle replaced the horse. The motorcycle replaced the bicycle. The automobile replaced the motorcycle. The driverless car may replace the automobile. Each replacement meant the destruction of previous forms of life, and this becomes interpreted as "progress." As the philosopher Terry Eagleton notes, "capitalist 'modernisers'" almost always "regard all change as positive and all permanence as negative." Yet this overlooks the truth that "some change is catastrophic and some kinds of permanence deeply desirable." He gives examples of desirable permanence such as French vineyards and a nonsexist society.[7] A society that values the virtue of truth telling would be a desirable permanence, especially in contrast to one that trades on alternative facts.

> Is truth only an illusory claim reflecting someone's invested interest?

Does society operate best when politics serves truth, or should we expect that truth is nothing but a mask of power, in which those "in the know" know that claims to truth are nothing but assertions of power that should be unmasked, generating a society committed to an adversarial politics of power? The latter answer would be the best one could do if nihilism

---

7   Terry Eagleton, *Why Marx Was Right* (New Haven, CT: Yale University Press, 2011), 84.

defines our culture. By nihilism I mean what the philosopher Friedrich Nietzsche (1844–1900) meant in his diagnosis of Western culture—that the highest ideals, ideals like God, truth, or goodness, devalue themselves over time. They do no work in the real world; they have no practical significance. If we think the truth sets us free, "Truths," he suggests, are nothing but "illusions which we have forgotten are illusions; they are metaphors that have become worn out."[8] What we once thought was true is now understood as nothing but an illusory claim to someone's interests.

Nietzsche denies that we, you and I, are really convinced that the truth will set us free. Take another look, he tells us, and you will see what the tragic poet Sophocles showed us. In his play *Oedipus Rex*, he questioned if the truth sets us free. When Oedipus seeks the truth for the cause of his city's plague, he calls in the blind prophet Tiresias. He asks Tiresias what the truth is. Tiresias responds, "How terrible—to see the truth when the truth is only pain to him who sees."[9] He would prefer to be sent home than to answer Oedipus's questions, and so he asks to be dismissed, but Oedipus insists. He must know the truth so that he can set himself and the city free. Later he says to his wife, Jocasta: "I must know it all. I must see the truth at last."[10] Tiresias tells him the condition of his own existence—he has killed his father, married his mother, his own children are his brothers and sisters. Learning the truth, Oedipus cannot bear to look upon it. It did not set him free, so he gouges out his eyes.

What should we learn from the poet Sophocles and from Nietzsche? One lesson might be not to seek the truth of one's own existence; you might not like the answer. It is better to live with our self-deceptions. A different lesson would be—seek the truth, but do not expect it to free you. Life is tragic. If we are to be

---

8   Friedrich Nietzsche, "On Truth and Lie in an Extra Moral Sense," in *The Portable Nietzsche*, ed. Walter Kaufmann (New York: Viking Penguin, 1976), 46–47.

9   Sophocles, *Oedipus the King*, in *Sophocles: The Three Theban Plays*, trans. Robert Fagles (New York: Penguin, 1984), 176.

10 Sophocles, *Oedipus the King*, 222.

free, it will require something other than truth. It will require the courage to look at our existence in all its horror without flinching. Both lessons question Jesus's claim that the truth sets one free. Truth does not lead to freedom. Truth has been devalued.

For Nietzsche, this devaluation of our highest ideals—God, truth, the good—is not a result of any conspiracy. It is simply what occurred in Western culture; it is our history. Appeals to former "high ideals" such as "the truth will set you free" no longer hold power over us. They have been replaced by advertising slogans, which show that we have power over them, and once we acknowledge that the truth is nothing but what we say it is, the truth loses its power. It is deflated, rendered nonmysterious. It is as if we have fallen through the looking glass and our words never measure reality; instead, they master it. Lewis Carroll noted this reality well in a conversation he crafted between Humpty Dumpty and Alice:

> **Have ideals been replaced by slogans?**

> "When I use a word," Humpty Dumpty said, in rather a scornful tone, "it means just what I choose it to mean—and nothing more."
>
> "The question is," said Alice, "whether you can make words mean so many different things."
>
> "The question is," said Humpty Dumpty, "which is to be master—that's all."

Words are tools we use to master reality, not discover or disclose it. Each of us has our way of using words to frame the world; and when those frames come into conflict, we have no rational means to adjudicate the conflict in order to come to consensus about what is true or good. We have no "local civic activism" that can deliberate reasonably over goods, especially when they conflict. We have only irreconcilable alternative facts based on data and an adversarial politics that uses data to manipulate the masses to our side. The only way to adjudicate them is through power, and not power in a positive sense—power to move one's self or to be moved toward what is true and good—but power in a negative sense, power as force leading to bullying, insults, coercion, threats of and the possible use of violence, even "the likes of which this world has never seen before." You have your facts about the world. I have mine. Who is to say which ones are true? And whoever that "who" is will not be some wise arbiter but the one who holds power, the one who wins. If this is the way the world is, truth will not set us free; only holding power so that we get to frame the world as we think others should see it will set us free. *Potentia liberabit vos*—Power will set us free, not truth.

There is much to be said in favor of Nietzsche's diagnosis of Western culture that truth is seldom innocent; it is related to power. We have too much evidence that some affirmations of truth are little more than veiled exercises of power. Yet, Nietzsche's diagnosis is not something one should affirm. If he is correct, then the world he describes will look like Martin Scorsese's portrayal of market society in his disturbing film *The Wolf of Wall Street*. It reflects late modern nihilism better than any philosophical treatise, and it is based on a true story, the story of another business leader, Jordan Belfort.

Nihilism and the Marketplace

Jordan Belfort represents the quintessential modern nihilist. Apart from his drug and alcohol abuse, his character shares much in common with Donald Trump—the pursuit of wealth, the degradation of women by viewing them solely in terms of appearance, a desire to win at all cost, questionable business practices, not necessarily hitting first but hitting back harder when someone hits you. Scorsese's film is based on Terence Winter's screenplay, which in turn is based on Belfort's autobiography. Scorsese's film is neither moralistic nor heavy-handed. He simply shows the excess of economic nihilism without ethical commentary. The opening scene in the film, taken directly from Belfort's memoirs (it would be a mistake to call them a confession; there is little remorse shown in his disturbing autobiographical tale of greed and excess), captures well the utter nihilism to which Belfort's fabricated Stratton Oakmont firm had descended. To encourage his employees, Belfort and the upper administration decided to have a contest tossing "midgets" wrapped in Velcro toward a Velcro bullseye. For Belfort, these people are less than human. In his autobiography, he admits that he has some reservations about tossing midgets, but his reservations are not based on ethical considerations. It is that they are "pound for pound . . . stronger than grizzly bears." Before he agrees to this dehumanizing act, only one of many that occurred daily at Stratton Oakmont including the regular degradation of women, he wants a "game warden who can rein in the little critter if he should go off the deep end."[11] Even after his conviction for money laundering, Belfort seems incapable of acknowledging the humanity of those he abused, swindled, or betrayed. He always had, and still seems to have, an economic rationale for his deceitful behavior, but what is most disturbing about his economic nihilism is that no rationale, no justification is necessary. One of his top administrators tells him that if there is negative press, they can justify the midget-throwing event by telling the public that they are increasing job opportunities for the "less fortunate." But, says the administrator, they most likely will never need to justify it because "no one'll give a shit."

"No one'll give a shit." It is inelegant, but it is a statement that explains the cultural context that made Belfort and his enterprises possible. It shows the same disposition toward the world as Trump's statement that he could stand on Fifth Avenue and shoot someone and not lose any voters. To put it in philosophical terms, both statements trade on nihilism. Truth, beauty, goodness, or logic, aesthetics, and morality do not matter. Nietzsche recognized and lamented that with nihilism the "beyond" would disappear in art: "With profound sorrow one admits to oneself that, in their highest flights, the artists of all ages have raised to heavenly transfiguration precisely those conceptions which we now recognize as false." An art with a "metaphysical significance"

---

11   Jordan Belfort, *The Wolf of Wall Street* (New York: Bantam, 2008), 67.

will disappear, and all we can do is narrate how it "once existed."[12] Nietzsche at least brought to our attention what was being lost. Belfort's memoir is as far from Augustine's *Confessions* or Dante's *Divine Comedy* as a casino is from a cathedral. When pilgrimages to casinos are more popular than pilgrimages to Santiago de Compostela, the artistry of a journey has lost any metaphysical or theological significance. To his credit, Scorsese captures this loss in his film. *The Wolf of Wall Street* is marked by its lack of beauty, truth, or goodness. Unlike many of his other films in which a metaphysical or theological significance can be viewed and pondered, no such gaze is possible in the retelling of Belfort's life. There is only vulgarity, manipulation, and vice. So, what is the point in narrating it? It serves best to demonstrate the incomplete nihilism Wall Street lets loose in late modernity.

The Wolf of Wall Street illustrates well Nietzsche's parable of the madman who announces the death of God. I think a case could be made that Trump represents our first truly secular president. Despite his appeals to religion, and the court chaplains who bless him, he clearly has little taste for religious matters. Trump has said that his favorite Bible verse is the Exodus passage "an eye for an eye." As John Fea, a prominent evangelical historian noted, "Trump was obviously not aware that Jesus himself, in Matthew 5:38–39, had something to say about the Exodus passage: 'You have heard that it was said "An eye for an eye, and a tooth for a tooth." But I tell you, do not resist an evil person. If anyone slaps you on the right check, turn to him the other cheek also.'"[13] Trump referred to "Two" Corinthians. He claimed he has never repented and is unwilling to apologize for anything. He views humility as weakness and is only attracted to the prosperity Gospel, a heretical distortion of Christianity that associates wealth with God's favor. It is no surprise that his religious advisor is Paula White, a prominent

---

12 Friedrich Nietzsche, *Human, All Too Human*, cited in *The Cambridge Companion to Hans Urs von Balthasar*, ed. Edward T. Oakes, SJ, and David Moss (New York: Cambridge University Press, 2004), vii.

13 John Fea, *Believe Me: The Evangelical Road to Donald Trump* (Grand Rapids, MI: Eerdmans, 2017), 3.

prosperity preacher who owns a $3.5-million condo in Trump Tower in New York City. As Fea notes: "It is very unlikely that Donald Trump would be attracted to a form of Christianity that emphasized sin, self-sacrifice, suffering, or anything else that might place demands on his life or prevent him from a pursuit of success as defined by his notion of the American dream. Donald Trump and the prosperity gospel are a perfect match."[14] If we asked Trump what he thought of a God who suffered and died on a cross, his response would most likely be similar to his response to John McCain's suffering as a prisoner of war, "I like gods who do not suffer and die, not weak ones who are losers." Trump worships the will to power.

Rather than the Gospel of John or the Letter to the Hebrews, what helps us make sense of our current situation and its nihilism is to interpret Scorsese's film via Nietzsche's parable of "The Madman." Trump's life, Scorsese's film, and Nietzsche's parable share a common context—the market is what renders life intelligible. Casino magnates are more capable of ruling than philosopher-kings, prophets, or priests. Like Nietzsche's parable, *The Wolf of Wall Street* begins in the marketplace, the trading floor at Stratton Oakmont. It exemplifies a basic premise in economics—value is created by creative destruction through the imposition of will. In other words, the world as it is lacks meaning or value. It is given meaning and value only when we impose our will on it. We do so by destroying old forms of life and creating new ones in a never-ending cycle in which the present moment is always disconnected from the previous one. *The Wolf of Wall Street* is a tale of "creative destruction," or at least a tale of disrupting economic flows and reorienting them toward the brokers whose job it is to disrupt them. Schumpeter's invocation of "creative destruction" was indebted to Nietzsche, so to make a case that Trump's presidency is best understood as a version of the nihilism present in market society, the opening scene of *The Wolf of Wall Street* and "The Madman" offer a good place to begin.

---

14 Fea, *Believe Me*, 137.

Creative Destruction as Nihilism: The Accountant's (Counter)Revolution

> Have you not heard of that madman who lit a lantern in the bright morning hours, ran to the market place, and cried incessantly: "I seek God! I seek God!"—As many of those who did not believe in God were standing around just then, he provoked much laughter. Has he got lost? asked one. Did he lose his way like a child? asked another. Or is he hiding? Is he afraid of us? Has he gone on a voyage? emigrated?—Thus they yelled and laughed.[15]

If I were to depict Nietzsche's opening vignette in "The Madman" in film, two obvious scenes would be either the opening scene of *The Wolf of Wall Street* on the trading floor at Stratton Oakmont or Belfort's first day on the trading floor at L. R. Rothschild beginning with the opening bell of the stock market. The two scenes are nearly identical. The pace is frenetic; the language is coarse; laughter, manipulation, degradation, and pandemonium dominate. All that is missing is a madman who seeks God in such godless places. He would, of course, seem completely out of place. Madmen seeking God belong in churches, not on trading floors. Placing Nietzsche's madmen in either of these scenes provides a sense of how odd the beginning of Nietzsche's parable is. Why has he come to the marketplace to seek God?

Scorsese is no stranger to seeking God. As he stated, "My whole life has been movies and religion; that's all, nothing else."[16] One would be hard-pressed, however, to seek God in *The Wolf of Wall Street*; religion and the quest for God are remote if not absent topics. There is no madman crying out for God. Rather than seeking God, it depicts a soulless, animalistic, secular will to power that reduces life to money.

---

15 Friedrich Nietzsche, *The Gay Science*, in *The Portable Nietzsche*, trans. Walter Kaufmann (New York: Penguin, 1983), 95.

16 "A Conversation with Martin Scorsese on Faith and Film," Fuller Studio, https://fullerstudio.fuller.edu/conversation-martin-scorsese/.

The term *God* is not absent in the film. The movie broke records in its use of vulgar language, and most invocations of God are for the purpose of cursing. There are a few parodies on prayer. When he first sees his second wife, while still married to his first, he prays, "God please help me. How can I fuck this girl?"[17] On another occasion, when he glimpses that his life is out of control because of his drug use, he says: "They say God protects drunks and babies. I was praying the same held true for drug addicts." Belfort hired a plane to retrieve him, his wife, and friends from a shipwreck, but it exploded, killing three people before it arrived. He interprets this as a "sign from God" that he needs to change his life. When the founder of Benihana's is arrested for money laundering, opening an investigation that would also lead to similar charges against Belfort, he questions, "Why would God be so cruel as to choose a chain of fucking Hibachi restaurants to bring me down?" After his arrest, he "thanks God" that his wife is waiting for him outside the courtroom. These are the only five uses of the term *God* in the film that are other than curses, expletives, or expressions of delight—"omigod." It is precisely in the absence of God that this film makes God all the more present. Scorsese shows us something similar to what Nietzsche demonstrated in his parable of "The Madman"—the implications of a world absent from God. It is a world of incomplete nihilism made possible by creative destruction.

Schumpeter is heralded for his unique understanding of the production of economic value through the role played by the entrepreneur and creative destruction. The latter term was not unique to Schumpeter. It was mediated to him from Nietzsche by way of the economist Werner Sombart.[18] The similarities between Schumpeter's analysis of the working of markets and Nietzsche's

---

17 All quotations from the film come from Terence Winter's screenplay. It can be found at http://www.paramountguilds.com/pdf/the_wolf_of _wall_street_screenplay.pdf.

18 See Hugo Reinert and Erik S. Reinert, "Creative Destruction in Economics: Nietzsche, Sombart, Schumpeter," in *Friedrich Nietzsche (1844–1900): Economy and Society* (New York: Springer, 2006), 55–85.

interpretation of Western culture are striking. For that reason, it comes as no surprise that Nietzsche has the madman announce the death of God in the marketplace. He arrives in the marketplace with his lantern early in the morning telling those assembled that he seeks God. They are enlightened businesspersons who know that there is no God, so they laugh, asking if God is lost, if he is hiding, afraid of showing himself to them, out on a voyage, or if he has emigrated. What is noteworthy about this opening scene is the utter lack of vexation on the part of the participants in the marketplace about God's death. The madman is tormented by its possibility and what it will mean for future generations. The assembled participants in the marketplace are unperturbed; they find it amusing. God may be dead, but that has no implications for their activities. Everything continues without the slightest hindrance.

One might say that the death of God in Western culture occurred not because of any heroic deed or revolutionary struggle. Perhaps it is best understood as the work of accountants. Schumpeter thought capitalism was the most dynamic form of economic production available to us, but it was unsustainable because of its cultural effects. Capitalism does not keep to its limited economic sphere but invades all aspects of life. Like Marx, Schumpeter thought capitalism was contradictory. Its contradiction was not found in a class conflict, however; it was found in its sociological consequences:

> Capitalist practice turns the unit of money into a tool of rational cost-profit calculations, of which the towering monument is double-entry bookkeeping. Without going into this, we will notice that, primarily a product of the evolution of economic rationality, the cost-profit calculus in turn reacts upon that rationality; by crystallizing and defining numerically, it powerfully propels the logic of enterprise. And thus, defined and quantified for the economic sector, this type of logic or attitude or method then starts upon its conqueror's career subjugating—rationalizing—man's tools and philosophies, his medical practice, his picture of the cosmos, his outlook on life, everything in

fact including his concepts of beauty and justice and his spiritual ambitions.[19]

The accountant is central in Schumpeter's analysis because he can place everything on a cost/benefit ledger that makes possible the proliferation of data and quantitative assessment. This subjugating logic invades domains that it should not, such as education, which becomes defined by outcome assessments and ROI (return on investment). It invades the family, with spouses and children defensible only in terms of the benefits they bring. It invades religion. God becomes an investment for which one expects a return—the basic confession of the prosperity gospel. Wealth and power become signs of divine favor. Once the value of education, family, or religion is placed on the cost/benefit ledger, they can no longer be what they once were. The "value" now given to them comes at the expense of what they were before. For Schumpeter, this capitalist logic is generative in economics but destructive in cultural spheres outside of it, spheres that are necessary if everything is not to be ruled by cost/benefit ratios. Capitalism contradicts itself because it destroys the very cultural values necessary for its longevity, devaluing them because of double-entry bookkeeping. The accountant's ledger subjugates everything to its instrumentalist rationality. God dies not from heroic acts but from the banal calculations of the accountants, from the desire to have this logic rule us politically and culturally.

It is hard to imagine that accountants are the source of nihilism, but Schumpeter identified them as the source for creative destruction, linking them to the term he inherited from Nietzsche. Because profits tend toward zero through circular flow, value is generated when the flow is disrupted through the ceaseless destruction of old forms of life. The flow fails to reach its course when an entrepreneur sees a new combination of the services of labor and nature and redirects them, destroying old and creating new combinations. What the entrepreneur interjects will

---

19 Joseph A. Schumpeter, *Capitalism, Socialism and Democracy* (New York: Harper and Row, 1975), 123–24.

eventually be followed by others, and in turn the circular flow will once again reach its course, diminishing profit to zero. Another entrepreneur comes along and interjects something new, and the circular flow is disrupted again, only to reestablish itself. Profit arises through this incessant destruction of old combinations and creation of new ones. It does not arise because someone creates something, but because they redirect circular flows. Each moment is completely new. Those who are unmoored from any past commitment—ethical, familial, political, or religious—and incessantly create "value" out of each new moment, always willing to begin anew by discarding the old, will be the winners.

Jordan Belfort is an entrepreneur bent on creative destruction. Initially involved in selling meat, his first company went bankrupt. He took the skills learned in selling and translated them into his work as a broker. After his arrest and incarceration, he leverages those same skills to become a motivational speaker. He sells selling. Belfort learns to leverage his skills at creative destruction from Mark Hanna, a senior broker with L. F. Rothschild. Hanna tells him that their primary concern is not with their clients but with redirecting the flow of money from their clients into their own pockets. They accomplish that not by building something or creating something but by selling an illusion. No one knows, Hanna states, "not Warren Buffett or Jimmy Buffett," what a stock will do.[20] Their task is to "pretend they do." They are selling confidence, a virtual reality, an illusion, and the point is to keep the illusion going until it cannot be sustained. The frenetic pace of moving from one deceit to another is how the illusion is maintained. "Look over there, not here" sustains the illusion; confusion and deflection are its main tools. Belfort takes these lessons to heart and leverages his previous life to sell penny stocks at 50 percent commission.

Belfort's worldview is nothing but that of double-entry bookkeeping; coming out on top, winning, is the only thing that matters. It is not inconsequential that he is the child of accountants. Early on in the film he describes himself in these terms: "My name

---

20 Terence Winter, "The Wolf of Wall Street," https://www.scripts.com/script/the_wolf_of_wall_street_44.

is Jordan Belfort. . . . I'm a former member of the middle class, raised by two accountants in a tiny apartment in Bayside, Queens." It is just a passing reference, but then everything is nothing but a passing reference in this film. It lets the viewer know that his world is the world of accounting. Belfort is not an accountant, but all his interactions embody the instrumental logic Schumpeter identified. His world is simple; it is about making sure the ledger always works in his favor, and that means turning everything into a commodity that can be placed on one side or the other of that ledger, including his wife and children.

Belfort gives us an account of his life. Notice the language he uses: "In addition to Naomi [his wife] and my two perfect kids, I own a mansion, private jet, six cars, three horses, two vacation homes, and a one-hundred and seventy-foot yacht." The hyperpace of the film does not give one pause to contemplate what he just said. There is no one who counters him by interjecting an ethical question, "Wait, did you just use the same verb to describe your relationship with your wife and children that you use for your horses and homes?" There is no time for ethical or theological deliberation. The next scene, the next excess arrives before one can take a breath—look over there, not here. Nonetheless, the language he used describes his cost/benefit rationality perfectly. His wife, like his children and cars, jet, horses, homes, and yachts, is a thing to be owned. When one thing grows old, replace it with another. All of Belfort's life takes place in the marketplace.

God is not utterly absent from *The Wolf of Wall Street* any more than God is absent in a post-truth society. But what "God" means has become so confused with other ideals that what "God" once signified has become devalued. Philosophers call this "incomplete nihilism" because those in the marketplace have not taken account of the metaphysical or theological significance of what they have done. It is incomplete because Belfort has replaced the "beyond" in art with a calculative rationality that was formerly recognized as a vice—greed (*pleonexia*), and that prevents him from seeing what is most obvious, the "cold breath of empty space" encircling him. Viewers see it all too clearly; for from the first scene we know where the film is headed. There is very little suspense, and yet the viewer cannot help but get caught up in a delight of destruction that keeps one's attention focused on what Belfort and his friends cannot see—that the destruction they gleefully wreak on others will inevitably turn upon themselves. They need a "madman" to point it out to them, to let them see what they cannot see. In one sense, Scorsese can be understood as such a madman, showing us what the world looks like when the horizon has been wiped away.

Incomplete Nihilism and Greed

> The madman jumped into their midst and pierced them with his eyes. "Whither is God?" he cried; "I will tell you. We have killed him—you and I. All of us are his murderers. But how did we do this? How could we drink up the sea? Who gave us the sponge to wipe away the entire horizon? What were we doing when we unchained this earth from its sun? Whither is it moving now? Whither are we moving? Away from all suns? Are we not plunging continually? Backward, sideward, forward, in all directions? Is there still any up or down? Are we not straying, as through an infinite nothing? Do we not feel the breath of empty space?[21]

The madman's quest for God ends in the marketplace. It is here, not on Good Friday in a worship service, that he announces Luther's famous line, "God is dead and we have killed him." He indicts the persons in the marketplace with murdering God and is frustrated that they have not recognized the significance of the deed that they committed. Nihilism describes that deed; it is when the highest values devalue themselves, when they no longer have any hold on us, when the term *God* becomes like the use of language Humpty Dumpty affirms: "When I use a word, . . . it means just what I choose it to mean—and nothing more." He decides what words mean. Trump has a similar reference to "God." Although any practicing Christian would know that the invocation

---

21 Nietzsche, *The Gay Science*, 95.

of the term *God* is intrinsic to the practice of forgiveness—"Our Father, who art in heaven . . . Forgive us our debts as we also have forgiven our debtors"—Trump has decided that the invocation of "God" has nothing to do with forgiveness. After telling us he never asks for forgiveness, he stated: "If I do something wrong, I just try to make it right. I don't bring God into that picture. I don't."[22] Just do it. Invoking "God" without bringing God "into the picture" is exactly what Scorsese shows us in *The Wolf of Wall Street.* "God" in the marketplace is like that; the term makes no difference.

Schumpeter did not invent the term *nihilism* to explain creative destruction. Nor did Sombart or Nietzsche coin the phrase. It was first used by the philosopher Friedrich Jacobi (1743–1819) against Johann Fichte (1762–1814), who radicalized the notion of will in Kant to such an extreme that it became understood as "the essential element of infinite and unrelenting self-assertion and negation."[23] Jacobi referred to this act of will as "nihilism." It fits well the economics of creative destruction and the plot, or lack thereof, of *The Wolf of Wall Street*—unrelenting self-assertion and negation define Belfort's life. The story line, inasmuch as there is one, is consistently interrupted by gratuitous sex, drugs, and dehumanizing activities. Most of it has no purpose other than the will to pleasure or power. There is only excess; unbridled greed consumes everything, including the proponents of unbridled greed. It is a depiction of life when the basest aspects of Wall Street are the social form of existence rendering everything else intelligible. We are all turned into voyeurs staring at its excess, knowing from the beginning it is headed to a very bad conclusion, but there really isn't any conclusion. It ends as it begins, with Belfort telling us, "Sell me this pen." We have gone full circle without making any significant progress.

The philosopher Martin Heidegger (1889–1976) picked up the term *nihilism* and distinguished incomplete from complete, or accomplished, nihilism. Incomplete nihilism is when the highest

---

22 The Editors, "Is God in This Picture?" *Commonweal*, March 6, 2018.

23 Michael Allen Gillespie, *Nihilism before Nietzsche* (Chicago, IL: University of Chicago Press, 1995), xvii.

values, such as God, truth, and beauty, disappear, but this does not change our values because the effort is to avoid nihilism by substituting some other value such as reason, history, culture, civilization, or humanity as the "highest value." Complete, or accomplished, nihilism is when "we meet the meaninglessness of the world in the wake of the diminished effective power of higher values not with denial and an overeagerness to revalue the world but with acceptance."[24] We simply accept that there is no truth, no goodness, no God. We give up the illusions. There are two forms of accomplished nihilism—passive or active. Passive complete nihilism ends in despair; it accepts the meaninglessness of the world through a resignation that says thus the world is, and nothing new or different will arise. Active complete nihilism, which is Nietzsche's position, is a transitional stage when one actively seeks the destruction of the higher values for the sake of "a whole new conception of value itself."[25] The higher values are not replaced with something else; instead, we move beyond good and evil to a different conception of value altogether.

The traders in the marketplace, in both Nietzsche's parable and Scorsese's film, represent incomplete nihilism. The highest value, God, has been devalued, but it makes little difference. They do not see what their own actions have accomplished. For this reason, the madman "pierces them" with his glance and asks them a series of questions. First, he wants to know how it was that they, of all people, killed God. Killing God is nothing short of drinking up the sea, wiping away the horizon, and unchaining the earth from the sun. To accomplish such acts, one would have to be a god, take on divine power for one's self. These are phenomenal acts of will, but the traders in the marketplace have met them with indifference. They laugh and carry on business as usual, throwing midgets at targets knowing that "no one'll give a shit" but failing to ask why, what has changed that we can throw midgets and no one cares? There is no vertigo, no sense that they have lost all

24 See David Toole, *Waiting for Godot in Sarajevo: Theological Reflections on Nihilism, Tragedy, and Apocalypse* (Boulder, CO: Westview, 1998), 37.
25 Toole, *Waiting for Godot in Sarajevo*, 37.

direction and that the coldness of an "infinite nothing" is pressing down on them. It has all become normalized, and those who sense the vertigo are the ones castigated for not going along.

Nihilism is incomplete when the highest values devalue themselves and no one is paying attention to its significance. The marketplace is the best site for incomplete nihilism because its hyperpaced, frenetic activity delays the attention necessary to see what has taken place. For the *Wolf of Wall Street*, reason as nothing but calculation of data now substitutes for the previously higher values. It leads to a self-absorbing greed. The spreadsheet has become the divine oracle. Belfort periodically emerges from his office to a waiting crowd and reads from it: "I'd like to read you something. Month end, March 1991. $28.7 million in gross commissions—all in Stratton issues. Not bad for penny stocks boys, not bad for dumpin' penny stocks." Having heard this word proclaimed, they respond with their "weekly act of debauchery," which is usually something dehumanizing. Belfort explains the trading floor at Stratton Oakmont this way: "It was a madhouse, a greed-fest, with equal parts cocaine, testosterone and body fluids."

Alasdair MacIntyre correlates the modern obsession with economic growth with the ancient vice of *pleonexia,* or greed. He thinks we have tamed *pleonexia* by reducing it to taking more than one deserves. This tame interpretation overlooks the depth of depravity *pleonexia* entails. It is a disposition to acquisitiveness in which "continuous and limitless economic growth is a fundamental good."[26] *Pleonexia* is the inability to be satisfied; it demands more and more until it consumes the subject of the one demanding. It is a constant state of discontentment requiring new acquisitions, whether it be spouses, jobs, properties, experiences, money. It has no end, either in the sense of "cessation" or "goal."[27] It never has enough. It does not rest.

---

26 Alasdair MacIntyre, *Whose Justice? Which Rationality?* (Notre Dame, IN: University of Notre Dame Press, 1988), 111–12.

27 See Oliver O'Donovan, *Entering into Rest: Ethics as Theology,* vol. 3 (Grand Rapids, MI: Eerdmans, 2017), 28–29.

Thomas Aquinas takes up Aristotle's *pleonexia* and interprets it as the "capital vice," to which he gives the name *avaritia* (avarice). It is a "capital" vice because it is ordered to a false happiness that cannot be satisfied, and thus it gives rise to many other vices. It is "capital" because it is an "origin" for these other vices, generating them in an ever-increasing multiplicity in pursuit of false and elusive happiness. Like all vice, it trades on a genuine good, the happiness that all people desire. There are "three conditions," according to Aristotle, for true happiness. It must be (1) "a perfect good"; (2) "sufficient of itself"; and (3) "accompanied by pleasure." It is an "excellence" that is desired, but there are conditions in which each of these go wrong, and "capital" vices are the result. Pride is the capital vice that falsely views the glory of the self as the perfect good. Gluttony is the capital vice that takes "the sense of touch in food or sex" as the excellence to be pursued. *Avaritia* is the capital vice that finds the accumulation of temporal goods, "assured chiefly by money," as the only object sufficient in itself. *Avaritia* generates other vices because its end is illusory.[28] Money cannot be an end in itself; it is only a means to something else. When it becomes an end, then it desires the impossible—"continuous and limitless economic growth."

The similarity between Thomas's understanding of capital vices and the demands made on us by capitalism are striking. Although economists like Keynes suggested that capitalism would create such an efficient system that the workweek would be reduced to fifteen hours, the exact opposite occurred. Far from delivering us from the curse of labor, capitalism has intensified it over the past seventy years. The workweek has become a nonstop global reality of 24/7/365.[29] Correlating dignity with work has only increased work's insatiable demands and, as Jonathan Malesic reports, led to disastrous consequences for modern life: "Lots of

---

28 Aquinas, *De malo*, 13.3, http://www.corpusthomisticum.org/qdm08.html#63244.

29 See Jim Edwards, "Why Tech 'Productivity' Is a Lie—and It Will Never Reduce Your Working Week," *Business Insider*, March 13, 2015, http://www.businessinsider.com/tech-productivity-is-a-lie-2015-3.

Americans have bullshit jobs, ones that have little tangible effect on the world but are nevertheless all-consuming, demanding that workers attend meetings throughout the day and chat on Slack after hours."[30] When economic productivity and continuous economic growth become ends in themselves, then they are capital vices. They require more and more of us until there is nothing remaining but the frenetic activity of productivity and growth. Jordan Belfort's life shows us the disastrous consequences. Belfort is *homo economicus*, nothing more. Scorsese is the madman piercing us with his gaze, making us look upon this reality. It is horrifying even while it is titillating, repulsive in its attractiveness. If there were no attractiveness to it, it would not work. Belfort tells us that the way he makes his brokers successful is by enticing them to be like him: "I need them to want to live like me." At the same time, the only way he can entice them to live like him is to make sure that his way of living is out of reach for them. If he is to elicit the desire for more from them, he must first acquire it himself and keep it out of their reach. *Pleonexia* knows no limits.

Nietzsche saw well the unremitting assertion of will present in commercial society. In his fascinating work *Debt: The First 5,000 Years*, David Graeber traces the origins of debt from antiquity. He debunks two myths about debt: First is the myth of barter, a myth present in Adam Smith and others, that ancient people did not use money but had a barter economy. In this myth, money becomes a rational instrument allowing for progress beyond primitive, barter societies. Graeber shows us that there is no evidence for this myth. It is a story we tell for self-justification. Second is the myth of "primordial debt." In this myth, debt is the origin of society. There was always money, and it was used to create indebtedness, which in turn gave rise to obligations that then make society possible. Nietzsche drew on this myth, suggesting that "barbarian law codes" that allowed cutting off body parts for compensation were forms of debt. It was this sense of debt that forms the imagination

---

30 Jonathan Malesic, "America Must Divorce Dignity from Work," *New Republic*, March 28, 2017, https://newrepublic.com/article/141664/america-must-divorce-dignity-work.

behind primitive communities. All of life is conceived in terms of debt and repayment, and it literally consumes the human body. As Graeber notes, however, Nietzsche's "premise is insane" and not backed by any evidence. The myth of primordial debt lacks evidence. Graeber suggests that Nietzsche knew this and used his analysis to show what the world would be like if the calculating rationality of bourgeois society truly was the basis for society.[31] Graeber's larger point is that it cannot be. Society assumes cooperation, not calculation. Accountants can never generate human societal bonds by the means of their trade.

> To imagine the world solely in terms of cost/benefit ratios overlooks the cooperative bonds that have value in and of themselves.

To imagine the world solely in terms of cost/benefit ratios requires an assertion of will that overlooks the cooperative bonds that make us human. When that happens, the world is understood primarily as an antagonistic marketplace where each person attempts to gain advantage over the other. Trumpism is the logical consequence of such a political imagination. Notice how baldly it is affirmed in a widely discussed op-ed written by Gary Cohn, then chief White House economic advisor, and H. R. McMaster, then national security advisor, explaining Donald Trump's "America First" policy: "The president embarked on his first foreign trip with a clear-eyed outlook that the world is not a 'global community' but an arena where nations, nongovernmental actors and businesses engage and compete for advantage."[32] Were Cohn and McMaster explicitly telling us that they, and Trump, see the world along the lines of Thrasymachus? The conservative commentator David Brooks suggests that this ideology explains the difficulty with contemporary politics: "Far

---

31 David Graeber, *Debt: The First 5,000 Years* (Brooklyn: Melville House, 2014), 75–80.

32 Gary Cohn and H. R. McMaster, "America First Doesn't Mean America Alone," *Wall Street Journal*, May 30, 2017, https://www.wsj.com/articles/america-first-doesnt-mean-america-alone-1496187426.

from being a band of brothers, their world is a vicious arena where staffers compete for advantage."[33] Brooks makes the case that this ever-present ideology gets human nature wrong; it assumes the normativity of selfishness, of greed, rather than cooperation. Graeber and Brooks, on this point, would agree, but Brooks over-looks how central this view of the world has been to the conservative movement he often affirms.[34] For that reason, he wrongly sees Trump as the exception rather than the consequence. What Cohn and McMaster described is not society or politics but the trading floor at Stratton Oakmont. If it becomes our politics, then it will be all-encompassing because it knows no limits, no end, no cessation to human antagonism.

What should we take away from Scorsese's film? What does it accomplish with its excess, hyperpace, and exhausting debauchery? If it is a form of incomplete nihilism, should viewers come away seeking to complete nihilism? Perhaps that is preferable than the unacknowledged incomplete nihilism that greed generates. But in the end, Christians should disagree with Nietzsche and Belfort's, Cohn, McMaster, and Trump's vision of the world. Even in this film with its intense attention to the dominance of the will to power, at least one moment emerges that cannot be rendered intelligible by its dominance. It is that moment, I will suggest, in which God appears.

Complete Nihilism or Beautiful Furniture?

> What water is there for us to clean ourselves? What festivals of atonement, what sacred games shall we have to invent? Is not the greatness of this deed too great for us? Must we

---

33 David Brooks, "Donald Trump Poisons the World," *New York Times*, June 7, 2017, https://www.nytimes.com/2017/06/02/opinion/donald-trump -poisons-the-world.html?_r=0.

34 Corey Robin shows how Nietzsche has been a longtime hero of the conservative movement in his *The Reactionary Mind: Conservatism from Edmund Burke to Donald Trump*, 2nd ed. (Oxford: Oxford University Press, 2018), 133–64.

ourselves not become gods simply to appear worthy of it? There has never been a greater deed; and whoever is born after us—for the sake of this deed he will belong to a higher history than all history hitherto.

Nietzsche's madman silences the incomplete nihilism of the participants in the marketplace. Atheism has not changed anything. The "greatness of their deed" goes unrecognized, and the madman leaves recognizing that he has come too early. They fail to realize that to complete nihilism they will need to do more than replace the higher values with something like calculative rationality or greed; they will need to build something completely new, completely different. For Nietzsche, that more is the "artistic taming of the horrible." One looks at the tragic reality of the world, a world that cannot be other than this, and one nonetheless says yes to it by willing it to be, primarily through art. Trump's vision is not near as grand as Nietzsche's, but it is related. After all, *The Art of the Deal* claims that "deal making" is an art. It tries to turn the antagonistic world of business into an aesthetics.

What would it mean for Belfort to complete his nihilism? Perhaps it would be to show us that the world is indeed as Cohn and McMaster asserted, an agonistic battle for comparative advantage. Belfort could show it to us just as Sophocles showed us the tragedy of our world in *Oedipus Rex*. Sophocles presents a tragedy in which everyone attempts to do what is just, and yet Oedipus still kills his father, sleeps with his mother, and his own children are his brothers and sisters. Oedipus cannot look upon such a world; he does not have the strength to do so. But in showing us this tragic reality, Sophocles also gives us something more, for we, as spectators, look upon it and, rather than fleeing the theater and gouging out our eyes, we are moved. We express how beautiful Sophocles has made this horrible tragedy, and that is what allows us to go on—"the artistic taming of the horrible."

Could *The Wolf of Wall Street* be read as a completed nihilism? Do Belfort's autobiography and Scorsese's film make Belfort's debauched life beautiful without blinking from its debauchery? For that is what it would entail if it were to function as an artistic taming. We would have to see it not as a comedy but as a tragedy. We would desire to look away and weep rather than gaze upon it and laugh. The only redemption would be to show us the tragic character of existence and yet give us an artistic vision that while acknowledging that this is the way the world is, and this is all that the world will ever be, we can find a way to say yes to it. But Belfort does not say yes to a tragic world. He does not even see that he is in a tragedy; his story is comedic, or better burlesque—a burlesque comedy, though, without redemption. Are we not living through something similar—a burlesque comedy that delights in destruction for no apparent reason?

Perhaps the most sinister moment in the film is one of the final clips. Belfort has spent twenty-two months in federal prison and paid $100 million in fines. After his release, he discovers a new way of selling things by becoming a motivational speaker. Just as he leveraged his failed enterprise of selling meat into his successful Stratton Oakmont stock brokerage firm, now he is going to use those same skills to sell us another illusory product as a motivational speaker—his expertise on selling. He has seen nothing, learned nothing, and made nothing beautiful. His final words in the movie return him to an earlier episode when he first gathered his friends to teach them how to be stock brokers: "Sell me this pen." He returns to the beginning, repeating the same line. There is neither decline nor progress, only more of the same, an eternal return.

The day Belfort became a licensed broker for Rothschild was "Black Monday," when the stock market crashed. Rothschild was undone, and Belfort was unemployed. He took a job selling penny stocks with Investor Center and realized that, given the large margins in penny stocks, 50 percent versus 1 percent for blue chip stocks, the accountant's ledger was clearly more on his side with the penny stocks, even though they were garbage, than it was with the blue chips. He also realized that the same skills his boyhood friends developed to sell meat and weed would translate nicely into selling penny stocks.

Belfort gathers his friends together at a diner to invite them to join him in a new venture, to start their own brokerage firm selling penny stocks. He instructs his friends in the "art" of selling by taking out his pen and saying, "Sell me this pen." Then, to sell them on the idea of selling, he says: "Every person you are on the phone with, they want to get rich and they want to get rich quickly. They all want something for nothing." Here is what makes possible the profits from garbage penny stocks. Everyone is a profit maximizer. His friend, nicknamed Sea Otter, interrupts Belfort's lesson, stating, "There was this one time I was selling pot to this Amish dude. . . . He says that he only wants to make furniture." After his comments, something powerful happens in the film—there is a brief moment of silence. The hyperpace of the film does not give many opportunities for silence and reflection. Everyone is always talking, hustling, dealing, and even in the midst of this chaos, no one reflects as to what he or she is doing. Their world is simplistically intelligible. People are profit maximizers, and recognizing that this is who people are allows one to leverage it for one's comparative advantage.

Sea Otter has momentarily complicated this world; he once met an Amish fellow whose purpose in life was not profit maximization but the construction of beautiful furniture. The friends do not get what he is talking about. One says, "I don't understand." Belfort also questions him, "What are you talking about?" Sea Otter explains himself: "I'm not putting words in your mouth or nothing but you just said that everybody wants to get rich." He is providing a counterfactual argument. There is at least one Amish dude who makes furniture to make furniture and not to get rich. He takes delight in the beauty of his craft as a maker of furniture. If this is true, then everyone is not a profit maximizer. The world would not appear as simple as Belfort suggests. Then Sea Otter provides another example, "Buddhists, too, they don't give a shit about money." Is it possible that there are people in the world who do what they do for something other than profit, who make furniture because it is beautiful?

Oliver O'Donovan argues that moral agency requires the necessity of an end. Without an end, there can be no practical activity and thus no practical reason. Like Sea Otter, O'Donovan uses making furniture to express his point: "A carpenter enjoys working with wood; but 'working with' wood involves designing and executing pieces of furniture; if one did not enjoy finishing a table, one would not enjoy working with wood. All acquired practices like those of crafts and professions depend on a clear idea of what counts as finishing a task. But there is no finishing without stopping."[35] Practical action cannot come to an end if there is no completion, no rest. Good practical action must come to the point where it says, "Look here!"

Neither incomplete nor complete nihilism, neither Belfort nor Nietzsche, can rest. There is no end, only a circulating return— "Sell me this pen." If *The Wolf of Wall Street* portrays the ceaseless "progress" required by capitalism, greed, and nihilism, then the only possible moment of redemption could have occurred when Sea Otter, tacitly proving O'Donovan correct, punctures that activity. Not everyone is ruled by what rules Belfort and his friends. Beauty, truth, and goodness have not been eclipsed. The fact that we can point to an end, an activity that finishes and brings delight to its maker suggests that there is still a "beyond." Here is a sign of creation that cannot be placed in the accountant's ledger, a work of art that is more than a commodity, something more than deal making.

But there is neither time nor space for thoughtful deliberation in *The Wolf of Wall Street*. After the momentary confusion that results from Sea Otter's comment, Chester returns us to their simple world by saying, "Man I could sell weed to anybody, get a convent full of nuns fucking wasted." If nuns can be sold something like weed, no one is exempt from Belfort's maxim: Everyone seeks his or her own profit. What if there is no one to buy furniture because it is beautifully and wonderfully made? What if there is no one who still delights in furniture as furniture? What if everything is placed on the ledger and understood only in terms of its capacity for economic growth, for the unceasing lure for profit? What if Chester is correct, and Sea Otter is wrong? Then there is no rest for there is no end, only constant activity, only the "art of the deal." If this is correct, then the best we can do is announce

35 O'Donovan, *Entering into Rest*, 29.

the death of God because there is no hope for Sabbath. But in so doing we should at least look upon the world as we have made it and be confronted with the difficulty of saying yes to it. Scorsese's *Wolf of Wall Street* at its best shows us that world and how difficult it would be to say yes. It is a post-truth world, however, and it appears as if many of our neighbors have become willing, accidentally or intentionally, to say, "Yes, give us that world."

Conclusion

"We need a businessman in the White House," so many conservatives and others said in 2016 and even before. The assumption seemed to be that the art of deal making would naturally translate into the art of politics. The resulting nihilism should make us take pause and ask if this statement has misled us. Of course, not all businesspersons are Jordan Belfort or Donald Trump, not all are nihilists—incomplete or otherwise. Yet the nihilism so obviously present in the White House would not have been possible without Trump's formation as a casino magnate and real estate tycoon. Like Belfort, he is *homo economicus*. There is a telling comment Trump makes about his children when they were little in his *Art of the Deal*. After telling us that he always allows them to interrupt him at work, he admits: "I've never been great at playing with toy trucks and dolls. Now, though, Donny is beginning to get interested in building and real estate and sports, and that's great."[36] Don Jr. was nine years old at the time. Like Trump, *The Art of the Deal* was not a fluke, some exception to an otherwise truth telling culture. It was on the *New York Times*' best-sellers list for forty-eight weeks, and for thirteen of those weeks, it was ranked number one. Undoubtedly, Trump "gamed the system" by having his own organization buy thousands of copies.[37] But the accolades and reviews made Trump's popularity. As a reviewer in

---

36 Donald Trump, *The Art of the Deal* (New York: Ballantine, 1987), 5.

37 See Alex Shephard's "Art of the Steal," *New Republic*, September 18, 2017, https://newrepublic.com/article/144541/art-steal-trump-boosted -book-sales-gamed-new-york-times-best-seller-list.

the *Milwaukee Journal* put it: "One of the most streetwise business books I have ever read. An unguarded look at the mind of a brilliant entrepreneur."[38] Trump was not understood to be an exception; he was heralded by the business community.

Trump's presidency represents a long trajectory in the conservative movement to remake the nation-state in the image of the libertarian corporation. We now know what that will look like: The president is CEO, cabinet members are his board of directors, or private employees, who are asked to sign nondisclosure agreements and noncompete clauses. The Department of Justice is a private security firm. Journalism should be its advertising wing. If it gets out of line, power is used to diminish it. It is derided as "the enemy of the people." The art of political deal making abandons any pretense of subordinating power to goodness or truth because all that matters is "value." That this long-standing effort culminates in Trumpism demonstrates that it has been the wrong direction all along. We should not be surprised that it culminates in nihilism, but we should not be pleased that it did so. Not only does it create a post-truth politics, it is also post-political. Chapter 3 attempts to explain what both of those statements mean. To do so requires a crash course in political theory.

---

38 See prefatory comments to *The Art of the Deal.*

GOODNESS AND A POST-TRUTH POLITICS

Chapter 1 asked if truth is a condition for freedom. It began with Plato's desire to subordinate power to truth and goodness but questioned if he had any remedy to do so well. Judaism and Christianity attempted a better remedy by requiring a truthful society in which bearing false witness is to misuse God's name. Chapter 2 looked at the consequence of a realist approach to politics and economics in which any attempt to subordinate power to truth or goodness is rejected. I have argued that this second history, a history marked by questions such as "What is truth?" and "What is a fact?" and statements like "alternative facts" and "truth isn't truth" better help us see what is occurring before our eyes. Trumpism makes more sense when correlated to Nietzsche's madman and *The Wolf of Wall Street* than to the Gospel of John or the Letter to the Hebrews. If the reader finds that juxtaposition clarifying, the next question is, How did we arrive at this place? If Trumpism is the symptom, how do we diagnose the underlying causes? This chapter takes up that question. It does so by clarifying what we mean by, and how we arrived at, a "post-truth politics."

As we consider whether our politics are post-truth and post-political and what that means, let us begin with another exchange that occurred on NBC's *Meet the Press*, this time between Chuck Todd and Rudy Giuliani. Todd was pressing Giuliani on whether Trump would testify before the special counsel. Like the previous example with Kellyanne Conway, the use of language in this interview quickly deteriorates to a point that makes it almost impossible to know what, if anything, is being communicated.

Giuliani: So, what I have to tell you is, look, I am not going to be rushed into having him testify so that he gets trapped into perjury. And when you tell me that, you know, he should testify because he is going to tell the truth and he shouldn't worry, that's silly because it's somebody's version of the truth, not the truth. He didn't have a conversation . . .

Todd: Truth is truth. I don't mean to go like . . .

Giuliani: No, it isn't truth. Truth isn't truth. The president of the United States says I didn't . . .

Todd: Truth isn't truth, Mr. Mayor, do you realize . . .

Giuliani: No, no, no. Don't do this to me.

Todd: Don't do truth isn't truth to me.

Giuliani: Donald Trump says I didn't talk about [Michael] Flynn with [James] Comey. Comey says you did talk about it. So, tell me what the truth is?

Todd: Don McGahn might know.

Giuliani: If you're such a genius—Don McGahn doesn't know. If that's [a] situation where you have two pieces of evidence. Trump says I didn't tell him, and the other guy says that he did say it, which is the truth?

Todd: At that point, you're right. Under two people. No. You are right. I don't read minds on that front. Let me ask you this final question . . .

Giuliani: No, no, no, no, let me finish. We have a credibility gap between the two of them. You've got to select one or the other. Now, who do you think [Robert] Mueller is going to select? One of his best friends[,] Comey[,] or the president[,] who he has been carrying on a completely wild, crazy . . .

Todd: Is it possible he makes a conclusion based on who has been more truthful over the years?[1]

Trying to follow the logic of this exchange is difficult. The key point appears to be Giuliani's claim that we never have the unqualified truth but only somebody's version of it. This claim is what the "politicization" of truth means. Claims to truth should be treated with suspicion because there is no unvarnished truth, only interpretations that serve interests. Todd has a more naïve version of truth: "Truth is truth," he asserts. Giuliani is not having it: "Truth isn't truth."

Giuliani, like Conway before him, has a point even if it is made poorly. Truth is not easy to discern. Two people have a conversation, and both come away with very different interpretations of what occurred. Neither may be dissembling. Instead, they misunderstood each other, or miscommunicated. The potential for miscommunication can, however, lead to "plausible deniability"—a way to dissemble without explicitly dissembling. One person, D, asks another, J, to do something that he knows he cannot explicitly ask. J thinks he knows what D is asking but is unsure because D's intention is unclear. Upon departing, each mulls the conversation over and at least two things could have occurred: (1) D was indirectly asking J to do what J feared D was asking. D wonders if J received his indirect meaning and will carry out his intention. J makes public what D was asking, but because D did not explicitly ask, he maintains plausible deniability and accuses J of lying. (2) D was not asking J to do what J feared D was asking, but J was convinced that he was because he knew D's character and knew that such a request was highly likely. J then makes public what he thought D was asking. J believes himself to be telling the truth. D objects that J's truth is not the truth of what happened, and D makes that judgment public. J, convinced that he told the truth,

---

1   Tim Harris, "Giuliani vs. Chuck Todd: Truth Isn't Always Truth, Comey's 'Truth' Different from Trump's 'Truth,'" *Real Clear Politics*, August 19, 2018, https://www.realclearpolitics.com/video/2018/08/19/giuliani_truth _isnt_truth.html.

responds by accusing D of lying. If Giuliani's convoluted judgment that "truth isn't truth" makes any sense, it would be because of scenario (2) above. In this case, J's truth isn't truth because it wrongly ascribes to D a claim D did not make.

The confusion made possible by plausible deniability reveals how important transparency and accountability are for truth telling. Giuliani's "truth isn't truth" takes what is true—that truth is difficult to discern—and turns it into a principle that can avoid transparency and therefore accountability as well. He takes shelter in the inability to discern between scenario (1) and (2). Truth, Giuliani states, is somebody's version of it. He does not qualify this statement. He could have said "sometimes," or "on occasion" what we have is not truth but "somebody's version." Perhaps if we pressed him, he would have qualified it. Yet as it stands, he set forth a principle that truth is never the unvarnished truth but is always politicized because it is someone's interpretation. That principle has some plausibility. Truth is a function of human judgment. There is no other form of truth available to us. Yet that truth is "somebody's version" of it cannot lead to the nonsensical statement "truth isn't truth," for that claim cannot be true without, once again, falling into the liar's paradox. If Giuliani is telling the truth—"truth isn't truth"—he is lying. If he is lying, he is telling the truth. When Giuliani then tells us that Robert Mueller will side with James Comey's version of the truth out of friendship and that makes him less credible than Trump, he doubly made truth political. If we can identify the interest served by telling the truth, it cannot be truth that is served but only the interest. Truth has been subordinated to politics, where politics is understood as the assertion of will, and this is what is meant with the expression: "politics is post-truth." If politics is a truthful deliberation about what is good, then a post-truth politics will also be "post-political."

Post-Truth Politics: Data and Politics in Service to Power

One reason for our post-truth politics is this common Nietzschean claim that truth isn't truth because it is always tainted with power. I will argue below that truth is always related to power, but this is not necessarily disqualifying because there are positive uses of power. There is a second related reason for our post-truth politics. Truth has been replaced with data. In an August 2016 editorial in the *New York Times,* William Davies opined, "The sense is widespread: We have entered an age of post-truth politics."[2] Our "post-truth politics," he suggests, did not begin in 2016; it has been in the making for decades. He traces it to the transition from "facts" to "data." Journalism and scholarly research are less concerned with discovering facts and more dependent upon gathering, mining, and assessing data. We now have immediate access to big data that shows peoples' sentiments toward nearly everything from the favorability ratings of politicians to the likely success of sports teams. But data, especially in terms of polling, is seldom "fact." Data offers a real-time glimpse into peoples' affective states. It lets us know what they feel about a particular issue or person, but not why. Data lacks narrative coherence, and facts make sense only when there is a narrative that can render them intelligible. Data can tell us that 46 percent of people polled approve of the president, but it provides no reasons. In that sense, our data-saturated culture fits well a moral theory known as "emotivism" (also called "expressivism") in which moral language is understood as "noncognitive"; that is, it does not make rational claims but expresses emotional sentiments. When we say, "X is good," we are saying little more than "I like it." The philosophers who fashioned this theory in the mid-twentieth century could be said to have anticipated Facebook, where moral and cultural debates take place by expressing one's preferences through emoticons. Perhaps these philosophers were identifying cultural shifts in the use of moral language more than constructing a moral theory. Data records what people want without asking if those desires are reasonable.

The two causes for our post-truth politics—(1) truth is always related to power, and that disqualifies it from being truth; and (2)

2   William Davies, "The Age of Post-Truth Politics," *New York Times*, August 24, 2016, https://www.nytimes.com/2016/08/24/opinion/campaign-stops/the-age-of-post-truth-politics.html.

truth has been replaced by data collection—reinforce each other. What passes for the use of the term *good* in emotivism also passes for what is true. It is what I, or we, like. If enough people are polled who express, for example, the feeling that a special counselor's work is part of a deep-state conspiracy or that it is important and must be completed, then the data is reported and taken to be the truth that matters for the moment whether or not either is fact. We record sentiments about data rather than deliberate about what is. The result is, as Rowan Williams noted, "the ersatz politics of mass theatre."[3] The result is that opinion is ever-present but truth increasingly elusive.

If truth is elusive, then our politics cannot but be post-truth because our lives are post-truth. It is interesting to note here that the thirteenth-century theologian Thomas Aquinas distinguished politics from despotism by suggesting that the former depended on rational deliberation and the latter gave free rein to desire without those desires participating in anything reasonable for which someone could be held accountable. Would Aquinas view our use of the term *politics* more like despotism than politics? Most likely. I am not suggesting that the thirteenth-century world was one of rational political deliberation and ours lacks it altogether, that despotism has replaced politics. Aquinas, for instance, thought that capital punishment for heretics was a reasonable political judgment. We do not, and that is progress. Reason is on our side, not his. However, when we use the term *politics*, as when a reporter asks, "What is the politics" of an action, event, or poll, the reporter is not asking for rational deliberation. She is not asking for the truth of the matter. She is asking how it will play with the base or the voters. She is asking for "data." That kind of politics is closer to what Aquinas meant by "despotism." It asks only, "What do the people want?" without asking if those desires are reasonable. As Davies notes, Trump is the symptom as much as the cause of this post-truth politics. We do not have to give reasons for our political

---

3   Rowan Williams, "Mass Democracy Has Failed," https://www.new statesman.com/world/2016/11/mass-democracy-has-failed-its-time -seek-humane-alternative.

judgments; they are expressions of sentiments like emoticons. He is what many of the people want, and it is not easy to discern why, to give and receive answers as to why this form of political life is good. This chapter seeks that discernment. I do so with some caution. The last thing I want to convey in this work is that there was a time in US history, politics, and culture where the virtue of truth telling was universally practiced and then, somehow, around 2015, or a few years or even decades prior, most people lost that virtue. Such a narrative would underwrite the nostalgia and sentimentality of "Make America Great Again." Nonetheless, if politics is to be truthful, it will require giving and receiving reasons for the goods politics should serve.

Political Goods

The question of whether "our politics" are "post-truth" assumes that we can speak intelligibly about "our politics," but a little investigation betrays how difficult that can be. We are uncertain as to what good, if any, our politics serves. For Aristotle, politics was, like ethics, a practical science, concerned with actions that make citizens flourish. Such practical action is concerned with what is good as well as what is true. The two come together in the virtue of "practical wisdom" where leaders know not only what is true but also how to act upon it by pursuing the good present in everyday life. Ethics and politics were related. Ethics occurs in the context of friendships; those friendships made up the *polis*, or city-states, within which the good can be pursued. If the latter were corrupt, ethics would suffer.

> Politics should be a truthful deliberation about what is good, not a manipulation of data for the sake of maintaining or accruing power.

Aristotle's politics are not ours. We don't live in small city-states where citizens meet in face-to-face interactions deliberating about what is good. We live in large bureaucratic nation-states in which fair procedures are supposed to allow each individual to pursue her or his own good. Such a politics makes it difficult, if not impossible, to speak intelligibly about a common good, or even common goods. If politics is deliberation about common goods, and we have no means by which to reason about them and arrive at the truth as to what they are, then we are post-political. Politics is not a truthful deliberation about goods; it is a manipulation of data for the sake of maintaining or accruing power. We no longer expect politics to have interest in truth or goodness. Politics is primarily about contending interests within an adversarial system. Trumpism's great value for contemporary politics is that he shows in full clarity what this system is.

Explaining all of this more fully requires a brief foray into political theory, and any such foray is fraught with controversy because politics, like ethics, is a practical discipline. Its definitions, judgments, and evaluations are not like mathematics. They are "somebody's version" of politics, but this does not mean that "good isn't good" any more than "truth isn't truth." It means only that arriving at goodness or truth requires deliberation and discernment; that is what makes it political and more than the will to power. I don't assume that the following account of US politics will be uncontested; it is my (I hope) reasoned deliberations that invite readers to deliberate with and against me as to what politics is, or could be, and how it relates to goodness and truth.

> **Arriving at truth requires deliberation and discernment; that is what makes it more than the will to power.**

Crash Course on Political Theory

Our modern politics is composed of complex and contested relationships among states and nations that include cultures, languages, uses of power, force, coercion, and violence—nonlethal and lethal—in an attempt to preserve and foster freedom. The *state* is the governing apparatus that is sovereign over a specified territory with demonstrable and protected borders. It is not the only "government" within those borders. In some sense, every community or organization within them has a government, a way of ordering its life to the goods that way of life pursues. This is true of the corporation as it is of a local bowling league. But the state government differs because it has sovereignty over all those forms of government.

In our modern politics, sovereignty is no longer invested in a king; it is found in "the people." But how "the people" can be sovereign is complicated. "The people" never gather and make deliberative judgments. Instead they elect representatives who make laws. Sovereignty is found in enforceable laws. This poses several problems. First, it forgets the original revolutionary act of violence that rejected sovereign law in order to establish a new sovereignty. Second, the new sovereignty prohibits the repetition of that original act of violence in new forms. Thus, someone like John Brown who raided Harpers Ferry in the hope of initiating a revolution against the slavocracy was not celebrated like the Founding Fathers but viewed as a threat to sovereignty and exe-cuted by it, reasserting its power. As Ted A. Smith notes, Brown raises the question of sovereignty because "he was right about so much." He was correct that "slavery was an abomination" and that "legal means were not going to break the system of slavery anytime soon."[4] Brown's case should make us ask which people constitute sovereignty and how they do so. Can it be something other than sheer power? I think it safe to say that sovereignty is invested in the state more so than the nation or nations, and that may contribute to the false assumption that it is power and not truth that sets us free. Let me explain.

The state forges together a nation either from preexisting nations, unifying them into a new national identity, or it destroys all previous identities to create a new national identity. The state is characterized by a monopolistic control over the means of vio-lence. Laws, a judiciary, police, and military forces are the main mechanisms by which the state functions and expresses sover-eignty. They are supposed to fall under civilian control through elected representatives who are also constituent elements of the state. The purpose of the state is government; the state governs

---

4   Ted A. Smith, *Weird John Brown: Divine Violence and the Limits of Ethics* (Stanford, CA: Stanford University Press, 2015), 20.

through institutions that enforce law. These institutions possess power, force, and potential uses of violence for that enforcement.

(The philosopher Elizabeth Anderson argues that corporations are also "private governments." Her argument is presented below.)

Power is not inherently negative. It is also positive. Power allows persons to be ethical agents.

Throughout this work I have lamented the fact that much of modern culture is primarily based on *power*, suggesting that there is something to the criticism that it succumbs to nihilism where goodness and truth are so devalued that they are reduced to nothing but assertions of will. Some differentiation, however, is necessary because power is not inherently negative. Power is also positive, something we cannot do without. At a basic level, power allows persons to be ethical agents. If we did not have the power of self-movement, for instance, we could not act. If we could not act, we could not be moral, cultural, or political beings striving for what is true or good. Truth and goodness do not simply fall passively from the sky; they are things we strive to attain in thought, word, and act. Power is the potential for self-movement toward what is true and good, and this is the case not only for individuals but also for collectives. The power of movement is not only individual; it bears an inescapable political aspect.

Consider the power to move oneself within the borders of a state. Such movement constitutes one of the important aspects of citizenship. Unlike crossing the border to a different nation-state, the power of self-movement within a state does not normally require special documentation. I have the potential to move from Dallas to Milwaukee to Los Angeles and even to Tijuana. At the present, I can move freely from Dallas to Milwaukee to Los Angeles, but I cannot move as freely from any of these places to Tijuana. It is also true that it is easier for me to move to Tijuana than it is for Mexicans to move from there to here. For this reason, the power of self-movement cannot be decisively separated from political ordering.

In 2010 I had a research sabbatical in Switzerland. I took my bicycle and went on afternoon rides. I would cross into France and Germany without even knowing that I had crossed a state boundary. While that power of movement was possible in 2010, it most certainly would not have been in the 1930s, and who knows if it will be in the future? Movement from place to place is a matter of politics, and for that reason, it should result from deliberations over what is good. One of the major crises we confront that has led to the difficulty of our present political situation is precisely this power of movement. We face a refugee crisis second only to the one that occurred after World War II. Failed states—failed because of unceasing war, economic hardship, and unrelenting internal strife—impose impossible living conditions. People are forced into an unpalatable decision: move or suffer. The power of self-movement to cross borders comes into conflict with state institutions that enforce law within borders. Mass migration generates fear in those who are the recipients of those movements, and that fear can be exploited for nefarious ends. Fear alone is never a sufficient reason for political decisions. If political decisions are made because people are manipulated by fear, then despotism overcomes politics.

The politics of fear calls for closed borders and the construction of walls. It limits the power of movement. Our generation is not the first to chant "build the wall"; it is a perennial temptation. In 1924 Clifford Walker, then governor of Georgia, gave a speech to the Second Imperial Klonvocation. This was a second large gathering of the Klan, whose resurgence had been sparked by D. W. Griffith's 1915 film *The Birth of a Nation* (more on its importance in a moment). The Klonvocation had similarities to the "Unite the Right" rally in Charlottesville, Virginia, in 2017. The purpose of both was better coordination among white nationalists. In 1924, however, some elected politicians explicitly affirmed white nationalism. In 2018 some elected politicians refused to denounce the white nationalists, but few explicitly affirmed them as occurred in 1924.[5] Walker, like the Klan, was worried about the easy power of

---

5   There was at least one locally elected GOP politician who explicitly affirmed them (see "How White Nationalists Are Trying to Infiltrate Campuses, *Today Show*, October 17, 2018, https://www.today.com/

movement from the south to the US, but his concern was not with Mexico but southern Europe, and especially the easy movement of Catholics into the US. In a speech titled "Americanism Applied," he stated, "I would build a wall of steel, a wall as high as Heaven against the admission of a single one of those Southern Europeans who never thought the thoughts or spoke the language of democracy in their lives."[6] Walker's fear was that southern Europeans were incapable of being integrated into the nation-state that was America. They were a threat to white, northern European, Protestant culture, which he thought was necessary to sustain democratic freedoms. The state needed to impose order on the nations coming to America so that the nation-state of America could sustain its common identity. It had to stop the power of movement through force, coercion, and, if necessary, violence.

> The power to move is intrinsic to human nature; the freedom to do so is a political and cultural reality.

While the power to move is intrinsic to human nature, the freedom to do so is a political and cultural reality. *Force* is a limitation on movement that one entity, individual, or collective sets upon another. Such limits can be legal or illegal, permissible or impermissible, natural or unnatural, good or evil. Some forces are simply natural and unavoidable. Examples would be gravity and the fact that two bodies cannot be in the same place at the same time without collision. There are carrying capacities to places that impose natural limits. Only so many people fit in an elevator. Others are cultural and vary among peoples such as forces that restrain others through intentional means. We keep people out of some places for specific reasons that should be acknowledged and discussed. Once those reasons are acknowledged, then the truth and goodness of those reasons can be discerned. If we keep

---

video/how-white-nationalists-are-trying-to-infiltrate-campuses-13462
18563687?v=railb&).

6   John Meacham, *The Soul of America* (New York: Random House, 2018), 119–20.

people out of our spaces from fear of crime or violence, a reasonable society would require evidence that criminality and violence are real. Otherwise such action plays into a long tradition of the politics of fear, raising the specter of despotism. *Coercion* is a limitation on movement that occurs against one's will either for good or bad reasons. A good use of coercion would also require the ability to give reasons for the coercion. Examples might be police issuing a ticket to a motorist or bicyclist for running a stop sign; tackling, tazing, or otherwise restraining someone to prevent them from engaging in harmful actions; arresting someone who had engaged in them; constraining children or impaired persons from foreseen dangers until they can deliberate rationally. *Violence* is the use of coercive means that do physical and/or emotional harm to another. There is a continuum of violent, coercive means between nonlethal and lethal terms. Because of the modern understanding of sovereignty, the use of lethal violence has become a state matter. Even "stand your ground" laws that put lethal violence in the hands of citizens require state authorization and adjudication for a citizen to use them.

The modern state attempts to forge a *nation*. A nation is much more difficult to define than a state. Nations are not necessarily made up of institutions that enforce law, and they do not control the means of violence. Political theorists offer different, albeit related, definitions of a nation. Anthony Smith defines a nation as "a named and self-defined human community whose members cultivate shared myths, memories, symbols, values, and traditions, reside in and identify with a historic homeland, create and disseminate a distinctive public culture, and observe shared customs and common laws."[7] Lowell Barrington suggests that a nation is "a collective of people united by shared cultural features (myths, values, etc.) and the belief in the right to territorial self-determination."[8]

---

7   See Brad Anderson, *A Chosen Nation: Scripture, Theopolitics, and the Project of National Identity* (Eugene, OR: Cascade, 2012), 31. I am indebted to Brad for helping me think through the relation between state and national identity.

8   Anderson, *Chosen Nation*, 31.

Both relate nation to culture, an exceedingly difficult and complex term. Raymond Williams referred to the term *culture* as one of the two most difficult terms in the English language, and he spent his life studying it, developing a sociology of culture.[9] Culture, he suggested, was a "noun of process" that became a metaphor for human development. Culture is constituted by language, practices, work, education, entertainment, and other forms of cooperative, human activities that convey a sense of belonging and identity. Nations are "regional cultures" that can be found within, without, or beyond state borders. A state may contain one or more nations. A nation's borders are less fixed, and more difficult to isolate, than those of a state.

Colin Woodard suggests that the US is not a single nation but, rather, a combination of eleven "regional cultures" that find themselves accidentally united into a single nation-state. The result is not harmony but an ongoing contest as to which regional culture will dominate. Nations exist without states, such as the Kurdish, Palestinian, and Québécois nations.[10] The Taiwanese and many First Nations in the US would be examples as well. Each of these is a distinct culture that lacks the governing apparatus of state sovereignty. These states do not control the means of violence within their boundaries. Nations without states are political entities, but they are political in a way that differs from nation-states. Some of these nations have been prevented from being states by the powerful nation-states within which they reside. The First Nations residing within the US had little say in the relationship between their nation and the state. Other cultural groups aspire to be a nation in control of the state, and such has been the case for white nationalists in the US for much of its history. In fact, they have had considerable control over the state, and that should register an ongoing concern about the truth and goodness of our national politics and culture, especially if you are from a nation

---

9 Raymond Williams, "Culture," in *Keywords* (New York: Oxford University Press, 1983), 87.

10 Colin Woodard, *American Nations: A History of the Eleven Rival Regional Cultures of North America* (New York: Penguin, 2011), 3.

that would be excluded by this kind of nation-state. Their recent reemergence is a cause for concern.

Rebirthing Nations

Imagine the following fictional scenario: A loyal member of ISIS who is a gifted filmmaker puts together a blockbuster movie that is a historical renarration of America, depicting American leaders as radical colonizers who have betrayed what makes America great by subjugating a superior people to rule by its inferiors. The superior members are radical Islamists and their sympathizers. The final scene of the movie includes ISIS members joined by other militias streaming into Washington, DC, with guns blazing, disarming the radical colonizers and preventing them from exercising their right to vote or hold office while Wagner's "Ride of the Valkyries" plays in the background. The movie is a huge success in city after city in the US. In fact, it is so successful that ticket prices are twenty times more than normal and the film still sells out. The president of the US, who is suspected of being a radical Islamist sympathizer and is a friend of the author who wrote the original book adapted by the screenplay, has a private viewing of the film in the White House. The film grosses $1 billion.

Although one might imagine someone like Alex Jones spreading such a conspiracy theory, it would take a wild, fanciful imagination to see such a scenario unfolding in the US. Yet this scenario is exactly what African Americans in the US faced after Reconstruction during the rise of Jim Crow. In 1915 D. W. Griffith, who had been raised as a Methodist, opened a hugely successful silent film originally titled *The Clansman.* Although theater tickets at the time were ten cents, his film was so successful that theaters charged two dollars. It grossed the equivalent of $1 billion today.[11] The title came from the third of Thomas Dixon's series of novels about Reconstruction and the rise of the "Invisible Empire," or the Klan, whom he saw as restoring the lost order of the southern way

---

11 See Richard Corliss, "D. W. Griffith's *Birth of a Nation* 100 Years Later: Still Great, Still Shameful," *Time*, March 3, 2015, http://time.com/3729807 /d-w-griffiths-the-birth-of-a-nation-10/.

of life. Dixon had been a fellow student and friend of Woodrow Wilson at John Hopkins University. Griffith originally titled his film *The Clansman* after Dixon's book, but after protests by African Americans led by William Monroe Trotter, a fellow student with W. E. B. Du Bois at Harvard and the first African American admitted to Phi Beta Kappa, Griffith did two things to make sure his film would not be censored. He changed the name to *The Birth of a Nation,* and he asked President Woodrow Wilson to view it in the White House. It was the first movie so previewed.

Griffith, who is known as the father of modern cinema, was without a doubt a brilliant cinematographer who used his talents in the cause of white supremacy. His work gave rise to a resurgence of the Ku Klux Klan. Much like white nationalists such as Richard Spencer today, he wanted to ensure that white supremacy had a place at the political and cultural table. He was very invested in free speech, the First Amendment, and "tolerance," not so much in truth—as we shall see. In 1916 he followed up *The Birth of the Nation* with a film titled *Intolerance* countering the protests of his film. During his time, art was not considered protected speech under the First Amendment. Most cities had censorship laws that kept certain things from airing before the public. Griffith made public appeals to free speech so that his film would not be censored. Trotter sought to censor it, appealing to the mayor of Boston, who alone had the power to censor works there. Trotter, who was the founder and managing editor of the Boston newspaper the *Guardian,* argued that the portrayal of blacks as rapists, second-class humans, and political opportunists who would use their enfranchisement to put the white race under their heel would lead to violence, especially more lynchings of blacks. He was right; it did.

The purpose of Griffith's film was to portray Reconstruction as a terrible and unnecessary oppression against white southerners and encourage the unity of whites from the North and South. It was an appeal to white civility against black irresponsibility. Northern and southern whites should be the real "nation" that was rebirthed through the blood of the Civil War. He cited Woodrow Wilson's own words in his film. In his history of America, Wilson had written that Reconstruction "put the white South under the heel of the black South." Griffith made sure that quote was displayed for all to see. It gave his film a presidential imprimatur (much as Trump's statement that there were good people on both sides did for some white nationalists at the "Unite the Right" Charlottesville rally).[12] The film originally opened in Los Angeles with the Philharmonic Orchestra playing the score. It then opened in New York City, ironically enough, at "Liberty Theatre." Although the film passed the censors, African Americans were not permitted to buy tickets for fear that it would lead to race riots.

The Birth of a Nation was aptly titled. Here was an explicitly racist advocacy of terrorist activities against African Americans intended to forge, through state power, a post-Reconstruction, unified, white nation. The film begins with the following quotation: "The bringing of the African to America planted the first seed of disunion." Disunion among whom? Among white people who should be united as a single nation and never should have warred against each other. It was an apology to whites that the war between them did not have to happen, placing the blame on African Americans, who divided them from each other. It portrays Lincoln as a friend to the South who refused to punish white southerners, unlike the Radical Republicans, who wanted reparations and the reconstruction of society so that whites could no longer dominate blacks. After Lincoln's death, according to Griffith, the Radical Republicans pitted whites against each other and put the South in the hands of blacks and mulattoes. These Republicans failed to see that whites should come together and form a national union without being divided by the inferior black race. Practices that would be taken for granted today—equality in terms of persons, politics, and marriage—are put forth as so horrifying that Griffith expects his white audience to recoil at their possibility, especially intermarriage. The conclusion to the film has the Klan standing guard to make sure blacks do not dare vote. Blacks are removed from political office and disarmed. The concluding

---

12 See "How White Nationalists Are Trying to Infiltrate Campuses," https://www.today.com/video/how-white-nationalists-are-trying-to-infiltrate-campuses-1346218563687?v=railb&.

scene begins with the statement: "Dare we dream of a golden day when the bestial War shall rule no more? But instead—the gentle Prince in the Hall of Brotherly Love in the City of Peace." Then follows a scene of a very white Jesus welcoming white people to come together in a peaceful union in his city of "peace." Griffith saw his film as antiwar, but it was selectively so. Throughout the film, he portrayed the Klan's terroristic use of violence favorably. The war of the Invisible Empire was necessary for the birth of the nation. He uses religion to tell a noble lie.

Griffith's father had fought for the Confederacy, but he died when Griffith was ten years old. Griffith's own relationship to the Klan and that of his family is questionable. In a 1930 interview he made a telling confession about the nature of truth that led him to produce his racist film:

Interviewer: When you made "The Birth of a Nation" did you tell your father's story?

Griffith: Perhaps I did. I suppose it began when I was a child. I used to get under the table and listen to my father and his friends talk about the battles they had been in and the struggles. Those things impress you deeply, and I suppose that got into the brain.

Interviewer: Do you feel as though it were true?

Griffith: Yes, I feel so. When you heard your father tell about fighting day after day, night after night. About your mother staying up night after night sewing robes for the Klan. The Klan at that time was needed. Yes, I think it's true. But as Pontius Pilate said, "Truth, what is truth?"

We have evidence that Griffith was not telling the truth.[13] As one biographer puts it, "Although around the time that *The Birth of a*

---

13 Much of this information, including the 1930 interview, comes from the PBS documentary *Birth of a Movement* from PBS documentary films, *Independent Lens*, http://www.pbs.org/independentlens/videos/birth -of-a-movement-full-film/. See also Meacham, *Soul of America*, 106–11.

Nation was released his son would sometimes claim Jake [Griffith, his father] had ridden with the Klan, there is no reliable evidence that he did so."[14]

Why would Griffith lie about his family's relationship to the Klan? Was he an opportunist who knew that white supremacy would sell? Was he a committed white supremacist who lied to serve the cause? Perhaps both are true. The cause is found in his retitled film, *The Birth of a Nation*. The title is politically and culturally significant. The US, of course, has been a nation-state for 139 years. Yet Griffith recognized that nations are not stable entities. They are birthed again and again. He used cultural means to appeal to state power to give birth to a new form of the nation, a power that President Wilson had already invoked by resegregating governmental offices. There had been a moment when a multicultural national unity might have been had, but Wilson did not have the vision to realize it. Griffith used art and culture to generate a shared myth that served the purpose of legitimating an evil form of the nation-state that abandoned the possibilities inherent in Reconstruction. It also had the indirect effect of initiating another movement of blacks for freedom. When many blacks saw what was occurring, they mobilized, creating an alternative movement with a different national vision. That movement was quashed for the next fifty years until the seeds planted in those protests gave rise to a potentially different nation in the civil rights movement. The tension between these national movements fuels America's present difficulties.

The forging of national identities can give rise to various forms of *nationalism*. Griffith's attempt to birth a nation is an evil form of it, as have been and are the various "America First" movements in US history. A crucial question before us is if national movements can ever be something other than a negative force. Although white nationalism and "America First" are negative examples of nationalism, not all national movements are negative. We have examples of positive national movements in the US such as the woman's

---

14 Richard Schickel, *D. W. Griffith: An American Life* (New York: Limelight Editions, 1996), 30.

suffrage movement, a movement that was present from the mid-eighteenth century in various locations until it became national in the 1920s. It extended the nation-state project to women who had previously been excluded from aspects of political and civic life. (Even riding a bicycle was thought to be improper to women until the late nineteenth century. It gave them too much power, too much movement away from the home.) Their commitment to the nation improved it, as did the civil rights movement in the 1960s by which those excluded from the nation-state project gained voice and vote.

There have also been other negative nationalist forces: White nationalism has already been noted. The Indian Removal Act of 1839 by the Andrew Jackson administration was a nationalist project, attempting to create a nation-state by excluding Native peoples and removing them from their lands. The "red scare" of McCarthyism was a nationalist project that sought to purify the US of all supposed communist sympathizers. Nationalism is negative when it privileges national identity among other identities, demanding loyalty and obedience. Donald Trump's inauguration speech sought to do just that. As Stanley Hauerwas noted: "Trump's inauguration address counts as a stunning example of idolatry. His statement—'At the bedrock of our politics will be a total allegiance to the United States of America and through our loyalty to our country we will recover loyalty to each other'—is clearly a theological claim that offers a kind of salvation. Christians believe that only God demands 'total allegiance.' Otherwise we run the risk, as Trump exemplifies, of making an idol out of some human enterprise."[15] One would think that religious people would readily recognize the idolatry present in negative nationalism, but this has not been the case in the US. The fact that many court

---

15 Stanley Hauerwas, "Christians, Don't Be Fooled: Trump Has Deep Religious Convictions," *Washington Post*, January 27, 2017, http://snip.ly/4bobk#https://www.washingtonpost.com/news/acts-of-faith/wp/2017/01/27/christians-dont-be-fooled-trump-has-deep-religious-convictions/?postshare=8331485536753022&tid=ss_fb-bottom&utm_term=.91e9772afd5c.

chaplains were there to offer prayers of blessings for just this kind of idolatry is reprehensible.

Christian Nationalism

Christian nationalists, especially the movement that emerged from Rousas John Rushdoony in the 1960s that is also known as "Reconstructionism," "Rushdoonyism," or "dominion theology" is a negative nationalism that holds power over much of the white evangelical church today. As Randall Balmer notes, it "seeks to rewrite civil and criminal codes to conform to Mosaic and Levitical Laws in the Old Testament." For some, this would include the death penalty for homosexuality.[16] "Seven Mountain Dominionism" fits within this same movement. It seeks to reclaim "seven mountains" for a Christian theocracy that include "family, government, arts and entertainment, media, business, education, religion."[17] A "Christian King" would be placed over each of the mountains. Larry Hutch, pastor of New Beginnings Church, claimed Ted Cruz would be one of the "Christian 'Kings'" who will transfer wealth from the ungodly to the righteous.[18] Pat Robertson, Jerry Falwell Jr., Richard Land, Robert Jeffress, and Roy Moore cannot be properly understood without paying attention to this US theological movement.[19] It has infiltrated the National Prayer Breakfast. This is not to suggest that they are all card-carrying Christian reconstructionists, but their theology, words, and actions fit within its ongoing agenda. Some current politicians at the state and federal level have been influenced by this agenda.

Christian nationalists found inspiration in Donald Trump, as they had previously in Ronald Reagan, which can be confusing. Neither Reagan nor Trump showed any hint of being Christian reconstructionists, but both recognized that this US cultural

---

16 Randall Balmer, *Thy Kingdom Come: How the Religious Right Distorts the Faith and Threatens America* (New York: Basic, 2007), 64.

17 Balmer, *Thy Kingdom Come*, 130.

18 John Fea, *Believe Me: The Evangelical Road to Donald Trump* (Grand Rapids, MI: Eerdmans, 2017), 130–31.

19 Balmer, *Thy Kingdom Come*, 65–66.

movement had a significant voting base and tapped into it. How Reagan accomplished courting the Religious Right remains puzzling, although his administration's support of Bob Jones University against the IRS over the question of interracial dating may have helped because that event, as we shall see, was one of the origins for the Religious Right. Reagan signed a bill that legalized abortion in California, was divorced and remarried, and showed no evidence of understanding or participating in regular practices of the Christian life. The Democratic candidate Jimmy Carter was adept in speaking about his Christian faith as was the Republican candidate John B. Anderson, a member of the Evangelical Free Church, whom Reagan defeated for the Republican nomination.[20] Why did the Religious Right choose persons less adept at their Christian faith than persons like Carter or Anderson? Many suggest it was the fear of the loss of power.[21]

Cal Thomas, who was an early leader in the Religious Right and close associate of Jerry Falwell Sr., later left the movement convinced that the seduction of power had led it to abandon truth. He wrote, "Christian faith is about truth, [and] whenever you try to mix power and truth, power usually wins."[22] The Religious Right has not listened to this counsel. It was, and is, a nationalist project that seeks to dominate the state in order to ensure privilege and power to their peculiar version of Christianity. It identifies the American nation with the Christian faith, drawing on "American exceptionalism" as a divine providential calling for America to be a "city set on the hill" that is an exception to all other nations. One serious problem with American exceptionalism is that it always requires an "exception" for America to be America—an enemy who must be overcome via extraordinary means. It creates a mythic violence at the heart of national identity: the Revolutionary War, the Civil War, the world wars, 9/11, and, of course, the ongoing culture wars. Real violence was suffered and inflicted in all those wars; that is not "mythic violence." What the violence

---

20 Balmer, *Thy Kingdom Come*, xvi–xvii.

21 See Fea, *Believe Me*.

22 Cited in Fea, *Believe Me*, 158.

supposedly accomplishes—birthing a unified nation and giving it a transcendent purpose—is the myth. A second problem is that American exceptionalism is idolatrous. The vocation to be a "city set on the hill" is a reference to Jesus's calling for his church, shared with the Jewish people and not with a secular nation. The vocation has now migrated from the church to America, secular-izing the church, turning it into a voluntary association in service to the state, and sacralizing the state.

The Religious Right fears that Christian America is being lost, that religious freedom is disappearing. We have heard quite a bit about this perceived threat to religious freedom over the past few decades. In fact, it is the basis for the origins of what has come to be known as "the Religious Right" in the United States. The accusation that religious freedom is under threat and the rise of the Religious Right are related because it has been this move-ment, not exclusively but predominantly, that accuses their fellow citizens of refusing to grant them religious freedom. The origins of the movement, as has been well documented, emerged from the 1971 Supreme Court case *Green v. Connally,* which refused to recognize institutions that violated the Civil Rights Act of 1964 as "charitable institutions." Thus, they could lose their tax-exempt status. Bob Jones University, which had not admitted African Americans until 1971 and forbade interracial dating after it admit-ted them, filed suit in 1975 against the IRS, which sought to revoke their tax-exempt status. The suit reached the Supreme Court in 1983, and the Reagan administration sided with Bob Jones Uni-versity in 1983. Paul Weyrich, an influential mover in the Religious Right and cofounder of the Heritage Foundation, admitted that rather than *Roe v. Wade*, it was *Green v. Connally* that energized the Religious Right.[23]

The origins of the Religious Right came along with the claim that religious freedom was under assault, and the source of this perceived threat was the desegregation of schools, especially pri-vate religious schools, due to the 1964 Civil Rights Act. Most of us, I hope, look back on these early claims and see in them not a

---

23 Balmer, *Thy Kingdom Come*, 14–15.

loss of religious freedom but a loss of the power to discriminate against and dominate others. There is nothing in religious freedom that should permit racial segregation, the opposition to interracial marriage, or the treatment of African Americans as second-class citizens. Without a doubt, the claim that religious freedom was threatened was used as a means to discriminate against others. The question that therefore must be asked in the face of accusations that we are losing religious freedom is, Are we repeating that error and using the expression of our faith to discriminate against and possibly dominate others? I am not suggesting that every subsequent perception of the loss of religious freedom will necessarily be related to a reaction against others' civil rights. I am suggesting that we must not ignore the history that renders that assumption intelligible—it is too baked into our national history.

Everyone should agree that claims about threats to religious freedom must not be used to underwrite racial segregation. Are there other events that might justify this fear? For some, undoubtedly, the fact that Christianity (usually Protestant Christianity) is not given a privileged place in US society is itself a threat to religious freedom, or even a sign of oppression. The accusation is made that America is a Protestant, Christian nation. We once offered Christian prayers in school, at sporting events, and so forth, but now, the argument goes, the secular leftists have taken that away from us. I confess that I bought into this line in the 1970s, when I was in high school. I led a movement to offer Christian prayers before sporting events as a form of evangelism. We received permission to do so, and I offered the prayer. When our principal, who also happened to be my father, discovered this, he put an end to it, claiming it was a violation of the Establishment Clause of the First Amendment. I came to see that he was right. We were not looking for religious freedom. We were looking for the right to dominate others, and because we were the majority in rural Indiana, it was easy to do. It cost us nothing.

Neither an effort to discriminate against and dominate others, nor to privilege one religion above others, can be a legitimate reason to claim a loss of religious freedom. Once we get rid of these two unjustifiable claims for religious freedom, are there others that might be justified? Let me offer some examples. I was baptized by the Anabaptists in Goshen, Indiana. They claim that violence is incompatible with Christian faith. Some of their religious convictions are honored; others are not. They are granted conscientious objection and exempted from mandatory military service, but they are not exempted from paying taxes to support the military even though this is a "sincerely held, religious belief," which is a phrase used repeatedly in the Supreme Court's decision in the *Masterpiece Cakeshop* ruling that will be discussed below. Some Anabaptists refuse to pay their taxes for war, giving that money away to other charitable causes. Their wages are then garnished for that tax. They are willing to suffer loss for their religious convictions. They do not create think tanks and movements to gain control of Congress and impose their convictions on others. They assume that following Christ will put you at odds with the powers that be.

Whereas pacifists are granted exemption for military service, just warriors are not. There is no religious freedom for those who are convinced that a particular war is unjust and that they therefore should not fight it; selective conscientious objection is not permitted. If the pope declares a war unjust, Catholics should not participate in it. They owe the church loyalty before the nation-state. However, this kind of religious freedom is not permitted.

The original rollout of the Health and Human Services (HHS) mandate was a threat to religious freedom because it did not grant an exemption to "faith based" and "mission driven organizations." The later correction to the mandate, which was affirmed by the United States Conference of Catholic Bishops, was, as they said, "a return to common sense, long-standing federal practice, and peaceful coexistence between church and state."[24] Unlike the Anabaptists, the Catholic Church seeks to have its religious freedom recognized by state power.

---

24 United States Conference of Catholic Bishops, "HHS Mandate Decision Represents Return to Common Sense," October 6, 2017, http://www .usccb.org/news/2017/17-180z.cfm.

Another example of a threat to religious freedom is the sanctuary movement, which privileges the bonds of baptism above those of citizenship. If an undocumented person seeks sanctuary in a church or elsewhere, this movement provides it. It works to keep families together even if the state has declared it illegal. Some persons have been prosecuted for their work in the movement.

The above cases are interesting conflicts between obedience to faith and obedience to the nation-state. They show the importance of conscientious objection, and I think it imperative that state government honors it. It is a testimony to religious liberty, even though it is often, as noted above, severely limited. What is granted the status of conscientious objection is complex. We should honor the religious convictions of the Anabaptists. We should honor the religious convictions of Catholics and others not to be required to support abortion. We should honor the religious convictions of Muslims and not use them to prohibit entry into the US. We should not honor the "religious" conviction of Bob Jones University and other forms of white supremacy to discriminate against African Americans. How do we discern when to honor a religious conviction and when not to do so?

The case that has dominated the Religious Right in its concerns about religious freedom is whether a baker who owns a bakeshop is required to bake a wedding cake for a gay couple when he finds gay marriage objectionable. The *Masterpiece Cakeshop* case raises a question as to what should be done when "public accommodation" to offer goods and services without discrimination comes into conflict with religious convictions. Since the Civil Rights Act, it has been understood that businesses that offer goods and services to the public must offer them without discrimination. Businesses are morally obligated to make public accommodation. The Religious Right emerged from concerns about how their "religious" convictions against interracial dating and marriage were threatened by that act. Once gays and lesbians were included as protected under the Civil Rights Act, these concerns surfaced again. Religious convictions also have a right to public accommodation in that they must be treated neutrally if those convictions are sincerely held. In the *Masterpiece Cakeshop* case, these two accommodations came into an irreconcilable conflict.

Let me begin by suggesting that Christians, and all people of faith, should have a commitment to "public accommodation" that offers equal access to goods and services for theological reasons, especially reasons of witness. After all, Jesus gives us the example of receiving those whom others thought were impure—tax collectors, sinners, prostitutes, adulterers. He did not require their purity prior to welcoming them. He did not require that they all repent, although he did require it of some. Even in those cases, he did not condition his welcome on their repentance. We should not say that Jesus was materially implicated in their sin because of his refusal. It embodies the fruits of the Spirit—peace, patience, kindness, goodness, gentleness.

If you own a hotel, you should offer lodging without unjust discrimination. If you operate a restaurant or grocery store, you should provide meals for patrons regardless of political affiliation. Likewise, if you own a wedding cake shop, and you are asked to bake a cake for a wedding, then it would seem reasonable that central to your commitment to public accommodation would be to bake cakes for weddings when asked. There may be exceptions. Perhaps you find your lodgers so objectionable that you cannot accommodate them without a violation of conscience. They might be white supremacists who want to rent your hotel for a klonvocation or a man-boy pedophile society that seeks to hold a celebration at your restaurant. While even these people should be entitled to shelter and food, not every aspect of their life should be accommodated. They should be resisted, and a conscientious objection clause be permitted that allows us to deny public accommodation. While I find that the above exemptions should be obvious, I acknowledge that other Christians find the same to be true of homosexual marriage, a conviction I do not share.

The question of whether homosexual marriage should be accommodated while white supremacists and pedophiles should not cannot be answered without addressing the truth and goodness of the moral and theological arguments for and against same-sex marriage. Jack Phillips, the baker who owned Masterpiece Cakeshop, most likely would agree with me that white supremacy and pedophilia should not be accommodated. I take it that he would not bake a cake that celebrated either of these, but he would include gay marriage in his list of actions not to be accommodated, and I would not.[25] We would need to deliberate and attempt to adjudicate our differences on these matters. I think there are convincing theological and biblical arguments for gay marriage, but that is not my primary concern at the moment.[26] My concern is not to engage in that argument but to ask when or if Christians should seek either judicial interference or legislative enactment to protect the freedom of their convictions, especially as they conflict with those of their neighbors.

A person of faith could abide by her or his religious convictions without any necessity to implement their objection through the state's instruments of force. He or she could, in other words, make a moral argument as to why they find accommodating a particular action, event, or person to be a constraint on their religious convictions without assuming it is the state's obligation to exercise force, coercion, and possibly violence to accommodate their conviction. The latter might do more harm than the former, so that even if the religious conviction is accommodated at the expense of the civil conviction, in the long run more damage is done to the witness to faith when it seeks to win by means of state power than when it lives from the power of divine communication.

Since *Green v. Connally*, the Religious Right has asked the state to side with it against those to whom it objects. Many of us consider that this five-decade attempt to couple Christianity with US power has done more harm to faith than accommodating those

---

25 I in no way intend to equate white supremacy, pedophilia, and homosexuality but instead find any equation of them reprehensible.

26 For an argument I find convincing, see Robert Song's *Covenant and Calling: Towards a Theology of Same-Sex Relationships* (London: SCM, 2014). My position, and how I came to it, can be found here: https://um-insight.net/perspectives/coming-out?fbclid=IwAR2JAPFYrjkpBE-_IbDVtelULB1FOHcj0527w0HA0OkQ51tqBpiGx4nDP8U.

objections. This consideration takes us back to Philo's defense of Moses's leadership. The normal means by which God gathers and unites the city made in God's image is through persuasive rhetoric, divine communication. If it can only be persuasive through an exercise of power, it is not yet divine communication building the city, and that leads to a politics of manipulation based on falsehood (see Psalms 147).

Through the Supreme Court, the state decided with Jack Phillips and against the gay couple, Charlie Craig and David Mullins. Truth had little to do with this entire incident; truth is not what concerns the Supreme Court. Understanding what is at stake in this case requires examining its historical context. It began with a long-simmering debate in Colorado going back to the 1990s, when the Religious Right tried to pass Amendment 2, which forbade elected representatives to consider including sexual orientation to protected civil rights status. They feared that gays and lesbians would be included under the 1964 civil rights decision and that would mean a loss of religious freedom. Amendment 2 was viewed as unconstitutional in *Romer v. Evans* in 1996.

The Religious Right was outraged over this, viewing it as judicial interference with the will of the people, but the people of Colorado did not favor Amendment 2. In response to the entire episode, the people of Colorado voted in favor of amending their civil rights laws to include sexual orientation. The Religious Right lost in both the judiciary and the democratic process. As David Opderbeck has stated, it was not the government that told Phillips to bake wedding cakes for gay people; it was the people of Colorado. Once the Religious Right could not create their nation through the people, they did it through the courts. They switched their approach from decrying judicial interference to welcoming it. Opderbeck writes:

> Following Romer, after much public debate, in 2007 and 2008 the people of Colorado amended the State's civil rights laws. That legislative result was unacceptable to the people who decried Romer as judicial activism, so now those same people cheer a different intervention by the Supreme Court as a

restraint on "the government." I'm sorry, but I can't help feeling that the absurdity of all this drama is worthy of Kafka.[27]

The Supreme Court overturned the decision of the Colorado Administrative Law Judge (ALJ) that was upheld by the Colorado Appellate Court (CAC). Jack Phillips had been required to make a wedding cake for Craig and Mullins by both the ALJ and CAC because the people of Colorado had democratically decided that discrimination based on sexual orientation was illegal and thus public accommodations could not be denied. Phillips appealed to the Colorado State Supreme Court, who refused to hear his case. The US Supreme Court did and found in his favor against the Colorado Civil Rights Commission (CCRC). The majority opinion found that the CCRC had violated treating Phillip's religious convictions with neutrality because members of the CCRC made statements that did not treat Phillips's religion with neutrality.

There were two objectionable statements. The first stated that religious convictions could not "legitimately be carried into the public sphere or commercial domain." The second was the following statement put forward by one of the commissioners: "Freedom of religion and religion has been used to justify all kinds of discrimination throughout history, whether it be slavery, whether it be the holocaust. . . . And to me this is one of the most despicable pieces of rhetoric that people can use to—to use their religion to hurt others."[28] These statements were taken by the Court as expressing hostility to religion, lacking neutrality. The first statement is deeply troubling. If it were conceded, it would require religion to be nothing but a private expression with no political or economic import. All conscientious objection on religious grounds would be dismissed, representing a secular

---

27 David Opderbeck is a law professor and evangelical Christian at Seton Hall University Law School. He wrote this via social media, and it is used by permission.

28 Supreme Court of the United States, "Masterpiece Cakeshop, Ltd., et al. v. Colorado Civil Rights Commission et al.," Majority opinion, 13 (October Term, 2017), https://www.supremecourt.gov/opinions/17pdf/16-111_j4el.pdf.

policing of religion. The second statement is simply true. Religion has justified discrimination. It has been used to support slavery and the Holocaust. It certainly should be questioned whether refusing to bake a wedding cake for a gay couple deserves to be placed on the same level as slavery and the Holocaust, just as it should be questioned whether asking a baker to bake a cake violates his religious freedom and oppresses him. If this is what the commissioner meant, his statement is rhetorically exaggerated. If this is what religious oppression has come to, no "Book of Martyrs" will be written anytime soon. But the Supreme Court justices were not interested in the truth of how Christianity has been and continues to be used for nefarious ends. It does not make rulings based on what is good, true, or faithful. That is not the Court's task; it must be ours. The Supreme Court asks only if "sincerely held religious convictions" were treated with neutrality, and in this case, they were not.

What constitutes a sincerely held religious conviction is not elaborated upon. Why is the religious conviction of a white supremacist not honored, that of the Anabaptists and Catholics are, and on which side of the ledger should we place Jack Phillips's request for conscientious objection to his Colorado neighbors' desire to include gays and lesbians under civil rights protection? I don't think we have reasonable ways to answer these questions politically because we cannot speak about what is good and true, which is why I fear we will see a curtailment of civil rights in the coming years.

The statements by the members of the CCRC were certainly unfortunate. They had no direct bearing on the judgments of the ALJ or the CAC. In other words, those statements were not mentioned at all. The fact that neither the ALJ nor the CAC denounced these statements was taken as their complicity in hostility to Phillips's religious convictions. The statements by a few commissioners that might be construed as hostile to religion were then assumed to be spoken even though they had no bearing on subsequent legal decisions. By not explicitly condemning those statements, the ALJ and CAC were accused by the Supreme Court of siding with them.

This ruling has caused concern because of the inconsistency of the Court. In another case, President Trump's explicit statement that banning persons from certain countries from entering the US was a "Muslim ban" was not included in the Supreme Court's ruling that permitted the Muslim ban. So, we have two uses of language: (1) A few members of the CCRC offered a critique of religion which is not cited by the Administrative Law Judge, the Colorado Appellate Court ruling, or the Colorado Supreme Court's decision. Because they did not explicitly denounce the statement, the majority opinion of the US Supreme Court ruled that they did not treat Phillip's religious convictions with neutrality. *What was not explicitly said was used as evidence for an intention to discriminate.* (2) President Trump explicitly and persistently called for a ban on Muslims entering the United States. His first few efforts at the Muslim ban were ruled illegal because they discriminated against persons based on their religion. Once his lawyers added countries that were not predominantly Muslim to the list of Muslim countries, the Supreme Court permitted the Muslim ban that was supposedly no longer a Muslim ban. *What was explicitly said was not used as evidence for an intention to discriminate.* I do not know how, or if, these two rulings can be legally coherent, but I don't see how they can be philosophically or theologically coherent.[29] They presume different accounts of intention and human agency. Associate Justice Ruth Bader Ginsburg's dissent to the *Masterpiece Cakeshop* ruling stated the problem well. She wrote, with Associate Justice Sonia Sotomayor concurring, "Whatever one may think of the statements in historical context, I see no reason why the comments of one or two Commissioners should be taken to overcome Phillips' refusal to sell a wedding cake to Craig and Mullins." There were several layers of independent decision-making that intervened between the commissioners' statements and the ALJ and CAC decisions. Nowhere did they give evidence

---

29 I've been told by a legal scholar that they differ because in the Colorado case the statements were adjudicatory and in Trump's case, they were executive. I still don't understand the difference and find it morally and theologically to be a distinction without a difference.

that the commissioners' possible hostility to religion played into their decision. Trump's explicit statements of hostility to Islam had no bearing on the majority Supreme Court decision.

While the Supreme Court admitted the statements of the commissioners as evidence of religious hostility, the majority did not do due diligence to the analogous case brought by William Jack that they cited throughout the judgment. When Craig and Mullins entered Jack Phillips's store, they were asking for a wedding cake to celebrate their union, something they assumed would be accommodated because they were in a bakery that sold wedding cakes. As far as I know, they sincerely sought his cake because of its artistic beauty. They were not attempting to make a political point. After the Colorado ruling against Phillips, when William Jack searched out LGBTQI-friendly bakers to bake cakes for him with antigay statements, he was not asking for public accommodation; he was engaging in political activities to manipulate the legal process.

William Jack is a well-known Religious Right activist who was so incensed by the original decision against Phillips that he targeted bakers and asked them to bake a cake for him with the words from Leviticus that describe homosexuality as a detestable sin. Jack has a radio show in which he once hosted Kevin Swanson, a known Christian nationalist who claims homosexuality should be punishable by death. Swanson also claimed that the Orlando shooting was God's judgment against "reprobates." This led Stephanie Mencimer to ask, "Did the Supreme Court fall for a stunt?"[30] While the commissioners' mostly truthful statement that had no bearing on the decisions of the ALJ and CAC was used by the Supreme Court majority as evidence for religious hostility, Jack's known hostility toward homosexual civil rights was completely ignored. It did not factor into the decision. No mention of it was made, but context should matter as we judge intention and material implication.

---

30 Stephanie Mencimer, "Did the Supreme Court Fall for a Stunt?" *Mother Jones*, June 7, 2018, https://www.motherjones.com/politics/2018/06/did-the-supreme-court-fall-for-a-stunt/.

To ask others to accommodate your religious convictions that refuse public accommodations to others' convictions would seem to be, finally, self-refuting. We have two conflicting claims that seek expression through state power. The first seeks state power—either through judicial interference or legislative accommodation—to protect their freedom not to be interfered with in exercising their religious convictions. The second seeks state power—either through judicial interference or legislative accommodation—to protect their freedom not to be interfered with in their exercise of daily life. The two requests, equally grounded in a negative freedom of noninterference, cannot both be accommodated. The resolution of the conflict can only be a rather arbitrary act of power.

Diverse and conflicting national identities compete for control of the state, each seeking to garner legitimation for its cause. Some of those causes are laudatory, and some are not. A negative freedom not to be interfered with is incapable of resolving the conflict between the two requests for accommodation. A different way to discern whose cause is laudatory and whose is not is the extent to which they foster truth or propaganda and demagoguery. Are they able to tell the truth about who we have been, who we are, and who we might be? Or do they falsify and/or forget the past and use any means necessary to impose their will on the state to secure their privilege against others? Our understanding of freedom needs some attention.

Civil Society and Freedom

Our crash course in political theory cannot simply address the state, control of the means of violence, and the nation(s); it must also address two other crucial aspects of our politics: civil society and the purpose of freedom.

Civil society is the arena of free, voluntary associations that do not depend on the state for their viability. It includes everything from the family, markets, corporations, sports clubs, unions, nonprofit organizations, charities, and so on. One way of explaining the difference between civil society and the nation-state is by comparing the consequences for exiting membership in an association of civil society and that of the nation-state. Voluntary associations are voluntary because one can exit them without serious consequences. If you ceased being a citizen of a nation-state—either by having your citizenship revoked or voluntarily terminated—there are significant consequences. In fact, you might be deported and not permitted to see your family, friends, or neighborhood again. If you exit a voluntary association within civil society, so the argument goes, the consequences would not be so dire. To leave one's family or a voluntary association might pose difficulties, but it would not result in deportation. In "liberal" society, and I mean by that a society determined by liberal egalitarian or libertarian freedom, one of the purposes of the state is to secure the freedom of civil society.

Freedom is primarily understood as noninterference. We consider ourselves free inasmuch as the government does not interfere with all those associations that make up civil society that are defined by the power of exiting without recrimination.

Liberal society is not the only way to order a common life (if freedom as noninterference can be viewed as a "common" life). There is also civic republicanism, which views freedom primarily as nondomination. We are free inasmuch as one group is not allowed to dominate another.[31] Liberal freedom did not challenge slavery because slaveholding states viewed their right to traffic in slavery as a freedom that should not be interfered with. Republicans at that time challenged it because of a different view of freedom. Liberal freedom and its sharp distinction between the state and civil society seeks to deregulate associations within civil society as much as possible. Republicanism has a less sharp distinction because it fears that the liberal, or libertarian freedom, does not sufficiently challenge domination.

One way that this has played out in US politics is with the *Citizens United* decision by the Supreme Court. That decision was a victory for the libertarian view of freedom because it designates

---

31 Although the Republican Party of Lincoln embodied, in part, this kind of freedom, the Republican Party of today is more of a libertarian party than a republican one.

corporations as persons with the right to free speech who can make as large a financial contribution to political candidates as they desire without public accountability. Corporations are persons within civil society who have the "freedom" not to be interfered with even if they have the power to dominate others.

Karl Marx argued that the distinction between the state and civil society led to exploitation. Marx, of course, is controversial in US society and for some good reasons. Marxist practitioners like Stalin and Mao should cause suspicion about Marx's teaching if they are its logical consequence. Yet Marx's critique is nonetheless insightful. If the sole purpose of the state is to use its sovereignty and governing apparatus in service to a liberal or libertarian freedom, then strong institutions like transnational corporations could have the power to exploit and dominate others. Those who consider freedom to be noninterference would see this as the price of freedom understood as noninterference. Elizabeth Anderson, who is no Marxist, makes a similar argument when she argues that corporations are private governments that have no democratic governance or accountability and thus are removed from political deliberation. Yet these private governments affect our lives as much as, if not more than, the nation-state. She writes: "Most workplace governments in the United States are dictatorships, in which bosses govern in ways that are largely unaccountable to those who are governed. They don't merely govern workers; they *dominate* them. This is what I call *private government.*"[32]

If Anderson is correct, the usual definition of civil society is called into question. It is not an innocent collective of voluntary associations one can enter into and leave without recrimination. Her analysis is similar to Marx's, but her remedy differs. For Marx, the remedy is that those who do the work in corporations should also own the means of production. For Anderson, the remedy is not socialism but codetermination, in which workers have a place at the table with boards of directors to participate in the

---

32 Elizabeth Anderson, *Private Government: How Employers Rule Our Lives (and Why We Don't Talk about It)* (Princeton, NJ: Princeton University Press, 2017), xxii.

corporation's decision-making, but the capitalist structure of ownership remains in place.

To understand the recent resurgence of democratic socialism among millennials, I think it is necessary to understand the relationships among the state, civil society, and the desire for freedom. As Corey Robin puts it: "The socialist argument against capitalism isn't that it makes us poor. It's that it makes us unfree."[33] The things that matter most about our everyday life are taken out of our hands. They are not only post-truth; they are post-political in the sense that we have no way of holding persons accountable for their speech and actions.

The rise of Trumpism in the US, as has been repeatedly stated, is as much a symptom as a cause, but of what is it a symptom? The previous discussion can now be brought together into a possible diagnosis. Like most political diagnoses, this one is by no means an exact science. The diagnosis is hypotheses that can only be tested over time; for if Trumpism is a symptom, removing Trump from office will have little impact if we do not attend to the underlying causes.

Conclusion: Hypotheses on the Reasons for Trumpism and Our Difficulty Telling the Truth

There is no single reason for Trumpism. It is bound up with concerns about abortion, religious freedom, gay marriage, immigration, the power of "elites," Supreme Court justices, and much more. It also results from five long-term developments in the US that made it possible: (1) the instability of a state-imposed national identity closely allied with white supremacy; (2) the misuse of religion to stabilize that identity; (3) the failure of our two-party system to address the real economy; (4) the conservative attempt to

---

33 See Corey Robin, "The New Socialists," *New York Times*, August 24, 2018, https://www.nytimes.com/2018/08/24/opinion/sunday/what-socialism -looks-like-in-2018.html?action=click&module=Opinion&pgtype=Hom epage. See also Corey Robin, *The Reactionary Mind: Conservatism from Edmund Burke to Donald Trump* (Oxford: Oxford University Press, 2017).

remake the state in the image of civil society; and (5) the cultural power of a small group of persons self-identified as the alt-right. Let me explain each in turn.

First, the United States is a state-imposed attempt to bring together diverse nations into a single identity that is so rife with tensions that the unity has been, is now, and, unless the tensions are addressed, will be unstable. The instability is particularly evident among those nations and their projects that are forgotten and excluded, especially the failed attempts to deal with the treatment of African Americans and Native Americans. These tensions were present between the nation's ideals and its practice of slavery. They erupted in the Civil War, which gave rise to the "rebirth of the nation," and then came to the fore again during the transition from Reconstruction to Jim Crow in the early part of the twentieth century, the civil rights movement at midcentury, and have returned in the practice of mass incarceration, which, as Michelle Alexander has so ably documented, is a new form of social control by which the US once again is trying to address the tension with a negative use of power that draws on coercion and violence. "Lock them up" was set forth as the answer to social problems long before "lock her up" became a chant at Trump rallies; it has become the new way we deal with the inability of the state to bring its diverse nations together at least since Nixon. No presidential administration since Nixon has addressed mass incarceration. It is an unstable form of social control and one that has generated tensions and will continue to do so if left unattended. Trumpism's critique of "political correctness," a term that is seldom defined, appears often to reflect a desire to forget or deny this history such that any mention of these tensions and their legacy is dismissed as special pleading or virtue signaling. The critique asks us to forget and not to face the truth, and thus to turn away from the possibility of turning toward what is good and bringing the nations together rather than letting one dominate the others.

Second, this state-imposed attempt at a single nation draws on religion as a nationalist project, which is why in the US we find practices that are absent in many other states that mix religion and nationalism like national flags in churches, the identification of national celebrations with religious liturgies, and a confusion of the secular with the sacred. Some of this goes back to the founding of the nation and the attempt to portray it idolatrously as "the city set on the hill," or the New Jerusalem. The US could be a witness to the force of goodness, but it cannot be and should not strive to be the New Jerusalem. Those who would try to make it so betray both the role of the church, which is the first fruits of the New Jerusalem, and the state, which should serve a legitimate secular purpose. Some of this religious nationalism is fairly recent. It was only in the 1950s that the US incorporated the words "under God" in the Pledge of Allegiance and "In God We Trust" on the dollar bill. The court chaplains willing to sing hymns like "Make America Great Again" in their churches are similar to Plato's "noble" liars who are either being used by this state-imposed nationalist project or are using its leaders for their own ends.

Those who don't fit are castigated, treated like scapegoats. Take the example of the former NFL quarterback Colin Kaepernick, who chose to kneel rather than stand during the pregame playing of the national anthem as a protest against the treatment of minorities by the US government. Anyone who knows the story of his protest knows that it is not meant to disparage soldiers, the flag, or the US but to bring attention to what African Americans face from the police and judiciary in the US. Any arm's-length analysis of the facts would suggest that they are on his side. Such protests should have an honored place in the US. After all, it was such a protest that gave rise to the US in the first place. Civil protests like Kaepernick's have generated positive transformations again and again in our history. They were first derided and later honored. Why, then, is his protest viewed as such a threat? I think it points to the fragility of a forced state project to create a national identity. When there is no persuasive speech generating a unified identity, jingoistic patriotism buttressed with unchallengeable symbols fill the void.

Evangelical Christianity was coopted in the 1970s by the Republican Party for the purpose of creating this state-imposed national identity. There has been a low-intensity civil war waged since that time, a civil war known as the "culture war," and so far the Trump administration is the victor in that conflict. Far from being an anomaly, Trumpism is the extension of a state project that began with Nixon's southern strategy of tacitly appealing to racism to bring white Democrats into the Republican Party, a project with strong evangelical support, continued through Ronald Reagan's foreign interventions and economic policies, and continued in part in the Bush and Clinton administrations. The Democrats have chased after the conservative white vote they lost since the 1970s, often neglecting all others. The result was an apologetic strategy to show they were as pro–law and order, pro-war, pro–free market as the Republicans. As Radley Balko has demonstrated, the Clinton administration, including Joe Biden, further militarized the police and contributed as much to mass incarceration as any previous administration.[34] The Obama administration did little to challenge this new form of social control. Former US attorney general Jeff Sessions's attempt to deter immigration by placing children in cages separate from their parents is a villainy beyond belief, but it is also an excess that draws on previous practices to use incarceration to deal with national tensions through state violence. It is both symptom and cause.

Third, Trumpism results from a failure of the GOP and the Democratic National Committee (DNC) to address the "real economy" and income inequality, another deep tension in the US. Given Trump's approval rating among members of the GOP—the highest of any Republican president in modern history—it makes no sense to argue that Trump hijacked the party. He is the face of a party that desired and exults in his leadership. Yet Trump won the nomination and presidency by offering bold promises to working-class people, especially white working-class people. (African Americans were told they didn't have much to lose.) On this point, Trumpism reveals a failure of the Democratic Party: it became comfortable with a plutocratic leadership that neglected workingpeople's lives. I am very doubtful that Trumpism will

---

34 See Radley Balko, *Rise of the Warrior Cop: The Militarization of America's Police Forces* (New York: Public Affairs, 2013), 192–237.

positively affect workingpeople's lives, but he was able to convince them that he had a plan to do so. Perhaps he does, but, like many, I think that plan is more snake oil than reality. As an article in *Forbes* magazine noted (a magazine as far in spirit from the socialist *Jacobin* as one could get), "America's Real Economy: It Isn't Booming."

Neither the increase in the Dow Jones under Obama and Trump nor the lower unemployment rates that both administrations can point to offer an adequate picture of the "real economy." They are data that can hide as much as they reveal. Peter Georgescu writes: "About 12% of Americans (43 million) are considered poor, and yet they are employed. They earn an income below $12,140 per year, and slightly more than that for a family of two. If you include housing and medical expenses in the calculation, it raises the percentage of Americans living in poverty to 14%. That's 45 million people."[35] Likewise, the economist Thomas Piketty has shown that the increasing inequality in countries like the US "has nothing to do with market imperfections. Quite the contrary, the more perfect the market," the more inequality results because the rate of return on capital "including profits, dividends, interest, rents, and other income from capital" is always greater than the growth of the economy.[36] In other words, profit from capital always exceeds growth in wages. Over time, this disparity increases exponentially. The inequality among the wealthiest persons in the world and those in the bottom quartile is now greater than it was under aristocratic regimes against which late eighteenth-century revolutionary upheavals were directed in the name of equality. The current income inequality is not a sustainable way to structure life together. Of course, Piketty and other

---

35 Peter Georgescu, "America's Real Economy: It Isn't Booming," *Forbes*, August 22, 2018, https://www.forbes.com/sites/petergeorgescu/2018 /08/22/americas-real-economy-it-isnt-booming/?utm_source=FACEBOOK &utm_medium=social&utm_term=Valerie%2F#2d3b277460b7.

36 Thomas Piketty, *Capital in the Twenty-First Century*, trans. Arthur Goldhammer (Cambridge, MA: Belknap Press of Harvard University Press, 2014), 27.

economists who share his views will be accused of offering "fake news." Think tanks will scramble to defend the system as it is. Data will be produced to counter his. Yet there is a simple way to get to the truth of the matter. Take a bicycle ride through the rural Midwest, Appalachia, or any major US city. See the blight for yourself. Trust your own eyes. Trumpism may be a sledge hammer used by some powerless persons to smash things as they are with an indifference to what is good or bad in order to see what might come next. That might be the best and most hopeful interpretation we have for the present moment.

Fourth, the conservatives' attempt to remake the relationship between the state and civil society has taken a strange turn, albeit one related to previous instantiations of conservative ideas, by adopting capitalism, something conservatives originally rejected. The original conservative movement reacted against the French Revolution, fearing that equality would diminish the virtues, especially the martial virtues that produced moral and political excellence. Beginning with Burke, this agonistic view of the world continues under different forms. One can see it in William F. Buckley's opposition to civil rights. In his famous debate with the writer James Baldwin, Buckley states that the equality the civil rights movement advocated would have the consequence of bringing down the white race rather than lifting blacks. Buckley stated something similar in his 1957 editorial in the *National Review* critiquing civil rights: "The central question that emerges is whether the White Community in the South is entitled to take such measures as are necessary to prevail, politically and culturally, in areas in which it does not predominate numerically? The sobering answer is Yes—the White community is so entitled because, for the time being, it is the advanced race."[37] Corey Robin has made the argument that what holds the conservative movement together is a reactionary logic that opposes liberation movements by subordinates against their supposed superiors for

---

37 Cited in Corey Robin, *The Reactionary Mind: Conservatism from Edmund Burke to Donald Trump*, 2nd ed. (Oxford: Oxford University Press, 2018), 51.

fear that a power to shape history through the most capable, talented, strong men or race will be lost. Conservativism is an "arduous struggle for supremacy" that exults in strength and power. It is why it so often opts for fear and power as the way to fashion the future.

Originally, conservatives objected to capitalism because it would destroy aristocratic privilege. The philosopher G. W. F. Hegel (1770–1831), for instance, feared that the dominance of commercial society would make people weak. He argued for the moral necessity of war to prevent the pursuit of wealth from taking over the state, turning it into nothing but a "civil society."[38] Capitalism gradually became a central conservative idea once the "successors" to the earlier anticapitalist conservatives recognized "that warriors of a different kind can prove their mettle in the manufacture and trade of commodities."[39] Later conservatives conceived the free market as a battlefield, a place of agonism where those who merit rule through their superior talents would dominate.

Robin's analysis of the conservative movement is not without its problems. His main thesis is that the conservative movement is an idea to preserve hierarchy even as the constitution of those hierarchies shift. It preserves hierarchy by cultivating a "reactionary mind," primarily reacting against liberatory movements. What is at one point in time liberatory becomes a new source of hierarchy at another. This makes for a confusing analysis. According to Robin's analysis, conservatives are for and against war, for and against law, for and against capitalism, for and against democracy. (He overlooks the central place for war among progressives.) Some of what he describes as conservative acceptance of violence is nothing but the virtue of courage. Yet his analysis, which was originally prior to the rise of Trump, is prescient in predicting something like Trumpism. It helps us understand two important points about the current conservative movement in its new Trumpian form. First, it explains why people who fear state power seek state power.

---

38 Georg Frederic Hegel, *Hegel's Philosophy of Right*, trans. T. M. Knox (London: Oxford University Press, 1967), 209.

39 Robin, *The Reactionary Mind*, 36.

Second, it explains the common refrain among some conservatives that we need a businessman in the White House.

Why are conservatives who are intent on limiting state power so adamant that they should be the ones who hold it? On the one hand, this is not a contradiction. They desire to hold and exercise the power of the state so that they might keep it limited. They supposedly seek power to prevent others from gaining access to it, who they fear would exercise it more broadly. They see themselves standing in the breach, keeping the forces of state power at bay. On the other hand, in order to possess and exercise this power they must take it upon themselves and use it—expanding it even while telling us it must be limited. Nowhere is that clearer than in the control of the means of violence. Large military expenditures, increased policing, including surveillance of citizens, the promotion of torture, the expansion of imprisonment, an increased military presence at the southern border against refugees, and the rejection of international law have characterized conservative policies since 9/11, if not before, often in the name of security. These policies vastly increase state power, especially as they are given a veneer of legality. We first expand the practice of violence, even torture, and then find legal ways to justify it.[40]

Increased and enhanced military, police, and judicial power is not the object of conservatives' fears about the nation-state. That is unequivocally considered necessary to secure the freedom of noninterference. Conservatives fear the state's encroachment into civil society, which is why strengthening the state's control and exercise of violence is coupled with fewer corporate taxes, deregulation, and opposition to environmental policies and labor unions. The state accommodates the libertarian view of civil society, reflecting its putative freedom as noninterference, but this ironically strengthens the power of the state. The strengthening of the state in its control of the means of violence serves to diminish the state's ability to interfere with the corporation. This diminishment may be illusory. Gary Dorrien argues that the freedom of the corporation in civil society from the state is an illusion.

40 See Robin, *The Reactionary Mind*, 84–86.

Corporations receive $140 billion in direct and indirect subsidies, which is a kind of centralized planning but one that is unaccountable to democratic processes: "Federal economic planning in the United States presently subsidizes the most powerful corporations and business interests in the country, largely on the basis of what has aptly been called the logic of the broker state. Since the giant corporations in the United States have the most means to lobby for assistance, they are also the chief beneficiaries of government loans, grants, import quotas, tax breaks, bailouts, price supports, indirect subsidies, uncollected taxes, and socialization of expenses and losses."[41] If Dorrien is correct, and he offers evidence that suggests he is, then Trump's interference in the market, picking losers and winners, is not an aberration but an intensification of conservative practice. Nor should we be surprised at the number of politicians who leverage their previous work in Congress for well-paid employment as lobbyists.[42]

Even if the ideal of the corporation free from interference by the state is an illusion, it remains a fundamental ideal among conservatives. This ideal helps explain Trumpism. Once people are convinced that freedom is noninterference and that this kind of freedom brings prosperity, a logical conclusion is that if we just had businesspersons who could implement this ideal in running the state, prosperity and freedom would follow. Despite numerous economists who have told us this ideal does not work, conservatism has an unyielding, dogmatic commitment to it.[43] The

---

41 Gary Dorrien, *Reconstructing the Common Good: Theology and the Social Order* (Maryknoll, NY: Orbis, 1990), 14.

42 See Lee Drutman, "About Half of Retiring Senators and a Third of Retiring House Members Register as Lobbyists," Vox, January 15, 2016, https://www.vox.com/2016/1/15/10775788/revolving-door-lobbying.

43 See Ha-Joon Chang's *23 Things They Don't Tell You about Capitalism* (New York: Bloomsbury, 2010), especially his "Thing 19: Despite the fall of communism, we are still living in planned economies," 199–209. Here his point is identical to Dorrien's noted previously. Chang's remedy, however, is not democratic socialism as is Dorrien's. He argues that capitalism requires saner regulations than libertarians acknowledge.

refrain that "we need a businessman in the White House" is per-fectly intelligible given the dogged conservative attachment to this ideal. Trumpism attempts to remake the state in the image of a perceived conservative ideal of the corporation within civil soci-ety. What matters is not truth telling, not even utility, but "value" where what is of value is not found in the world, for the world in itself is meaningless, lying there as neutral, raw resources until we give them value. We give them value not through labor but through the will of the strongman, the CEO who knows the art of the deal.

The loss of truth and goodness in the world is tied to a theory of value that has taken hold in Western culture since the rise of the Austrian school of economics. At least with the British utilitarians, "utility" could be found in the objects in the world that satisfied the needs of agents. For John Stuart Mill, utility required a "dig-nity" in persons and things that would find satisfaction in things that are more noble. Bentham's utilitarianism did not hold to Mill's assumption of a "qualitative" ordering of values. He related utility solely to the quantitative satisfaction of needs without judgment about the objects that satisfied those needs. With Mill's qualitative utilitarianism, objects could be rank ordered based on their partic-ipation in dignity. (Whether that is still a version of utilitarian ethics is questionable.) After Austrian economists emphasized consumer preference, value became completely subjective. The world as it is lacks any meaning. The only meaning it has is the meaning we give to it. Carl Menger stated it thus: "Value is therefore nothing inherent in goods, no property of them, but merely the impor-tance that we first attribute to the satisfaction of our needs, that is, to our lives and well-being."[44] Menger distinguished his theory of value from utilitarianism because in it an object in the world still has utility that satisfied the need of the agent. In contrast to it, for Menger, objects are meaningless until the will gives them value by its choices. Of course, as I argued in chapter 2, this theory of value is nearly identical to Nietzsche's. He, too, stated explicitly

---

44 Cited in Robin, *The Reactionary Mind*, 146.

that value "is entirely subjective in nature."[45] I find this theory of value helpful in clarifying Trump's obviously contradictory statements. We see him mock a person who has a disability. It is before our eyes. Pressed about it, he says that he did not do what we saw him do. His contradictory tweets are so blatant that they are hard to explain. But if the world is meaningless until the strongman, the CEO, gives it value, then the contradictions are clarified. What is true or good is a function of the will in each moment it gives value to otherwise inert objects in the world. Trump's confusing actions make sense within the subjective theory of value that has dominated the conservative tradition since the rise of the Austrian school, a school that turned market relations into a morality.

Fifth, this diagnosis should not be neglected; it is one that is related to the first point noted above: the rise of the alt-right in our national politics and their ability to gain a significant voice in the cultural conversation. I do not want to give this movement more attention than it deserves, but it undoubtedly had an influence in 2016. Like many others, I had not been paying attention to the alt-right prior to that time. I had never read Breitbart News; nor did I know who Steve Bannon, Stephen Miller, or Milo Yiannoupolis were. I thought green frogs were decorative ornaments for gardens; since 2016 I have discovered otherwise. I now know they are the symbol for a new white supremacy movement.

Yiannoupolis and Allum Bokhari wrote an essay for Breitbart in March 2016 titled "An Establishment Conservative's Guide to the Alt-Right" that is informative about the emergence of the alt-right. Establishment conservatives are the alt-right's enemy, so this essay was something of a warning. The alt-right was a previous subculture that rose to prominence to threaten not only "progressives" but also other conservatives. They wrote: "Previously an obscure subculture, the alt-right burst onto the national political scene in 2015. Although initially small in number, the alt-right has a youthful energy and jarring, taboo-defying rhetoric that have

---

45 Robin, *The Reactionary Mind*, 147–48.

boosted its membership and made it impossible to ignore."[46] Constant attacks on "political correctness" constitute the taboo-defying rhetoric. Anti-Semitic, antigay, antiblack, anti-elite, anti-neoliberalism, and anti-establishment rhetoric is promulgated by persons who are Jewish, gay, and clearly part of the elite, having been educated at many of the nation's elite universities. A dominant drive of the alt-right is to preserve European culture, which they see as under threat from immigrants and refugees, especially from Islamic nations. Yiannopoulos and Bokhari state that the news media, universities, and the elites have treated this desire to preserve European culture as racist: "For decades, the concern of those who cherish Western culture have been openly ridiculed and dismissed as racist." They provide no evidence that this is the case, but it is one of the reasons that they provoke progressives with intentionally racist and anti-Semitic language. It is less about racism, they suggest, than transgressing norms that they find to be censoring free speech. They are ardent devotees of the First Amendment.

The alt-right is explicitly pro-Russia and anti-China. Russia represents a strong nation that has defied political correctness by its prohibitions against homosexuality and its commitment to white Europeans. Several of the most extreme alt-right white nationalists have praised Russia such as Matthew Heimbach, Richard Spencer, and David Duke. Spencer, an avowed white nationalist, started a think tank called the National Policy Institute that encourages the US to leave NATO, establish a new relationship with Russia, and embrace Syria's President Bashar al-Asaad. He referred to Russia as "the sole white power in the world." David Duke maintains a residence in Russia, which he has used to "promote" his anti-Semitic book and agenda.[47] Some members of the alt-right are

---

46 Allum Bokhari and Milo Yiannopoulous, "An Establishment Conservative's Guide to the Alt-Right," Breitbart, March 29, 2016, http://www.breitbart.com/tech/2016/03/29/an-establishment-conservatives-guide-to-the-alt-right/.
47 Natasha Bertrand, "'A Model for Civilization': Putin's Russia Has Emerged as 'a Beacon for Nationalists' and the American Alt-Right,"

explicitly white nationalists. They make a feeble attempt to distance their nationalism from white supremacy by suggesting that they also believe in self-determination for other ethnic groups. They affirm black and Native American nationalism. The alt-right also advocates for strong military and policing. How influential is the alt-right in our current culture? The similarity between much of what they advocate and what has been implemented by Trump and Sessions is striking. Yet, I don't think the alt-right should be credited with more influence and power than they deserve. They feel emboldened by the Trump presidency and have explicitly said so. Trump and Sessions refuse to take any blame for their more visible presence in US culture since 2016, and they reject any direct connection to them, but at least one of them has spoken at a Trump rally.[48] Even if their influence is minimal and/or indirect, the emergence of the alt-right as a political force and the legacy of white supremacy should raise alarms.

These five trajectories inhibit the virtue of truth telling:

The first keeps us from seeing our past as it is. We manufacture deceptions about our history that we then inhabit.

The second offers religious legitimation for those deceptions. These two contribute to the neglect of a serious analysis of the real economy.

The third may be the most important reason for Trumpism's rise, but Trumpism has not, and most likely will not, do more than continue to divert attention from the legitimate grievances of the white working class.

The fourth replaces truth with utility or value. It has the potential to do the most long-lasting damage to our culture.

The fifth is alarming. The alt-right is explicitly nihilist. Everything held dear—truth, God, goodness—will die at their hands; their

---

Business Insider, December 10, 2016, https://www.businessinsider.com/russia-connections-to-the-alt-right-2016-11.

48 See "How White Nationalists Are Trying to Infiltrate Campuses," https://www.today.com/video/how-white-nationalists-are-trying-to-infiltrate-campuses-1346218563687?v=railb&.

influence, hopefully, will soon pass. They still have people in high administrative places, and that should continue to cause concern.

Trump's rallies are a logical conclusion to the five trajectories outlined in this chapter. They express what remains of "politics" when truth and deliberation over goods are excluded. We are left with chants, sloganeering, protests, and vicious displays of power against each other—"Lock her, him, or them up," "Body slam them," "Punch them in the face," "These are the enemies of the people." Every action causes a reaction. "I'd take him behind the gym and beat the hell out of him." "When they go low, we kick them." The vicious cycle spirals downward; it has no bottom. A post-political politics diminishes us all. If we cannot figure out how to tell the truth in charity, it cannot end well. Do you not feel the weight of what is coming if something does not change? Perhaps it is already here, or always has been, waiting in the wings, and what haunts us returns because we became inattentive to it, inattentive to our susceptibility to the lie.

THE VIRTUE OF TRUTH TELLING AND THE ECCLESIAL APPROACH

Given the three previous chapters, what should we do? First, practice the virtue of truth telling, so we might discover if it sets us free, even from our present situation. That will require at least a basic understanding of truth, which is no small matter. Truth is complicated. That is why appeals to "alternative facts" and statements like "truth isn't truth" have a certain plausibility. Questioning the possibility of truth is easy. Not expecting an answer to the question "What is truth?" and dismissing the question altogether is even easier. The complexity of truth is why it can so easily be replaced with power and advantage—they are not complicated. But if we are to sustain the claim that truth is more freeing than power, we must be able to give reasons why.

> The complexity of truth is why it can so easily be replaced with power and advantage— they are not complicated.

The Virtue and Metaphysics of Truth

We can begin to answer the question "What is truth?" with a basic definition of truth found from the ancient philosopher Aristotle through the medieval theologian Thomas Aquinas, one that I have cited in previous chapters: "To say of what is that it is or of what is not that it is not is true. To say of what is that it is not or to say of what is not that it is is false." That answer does not resolve the difficult question of "What is truth?" but it initiates a proper inquiry. It does not raise the question in order to dismiss it. It does not hide behind "alternative facts" or claim that truth isn't truth but only somebody's version of it. Aristotle's definition at least points us in the right direction of retrieving the virtue of truth telling. I will exegete this definition by examining its constituent parts.

"To say of . . ."

The first thing to note about this definition is that truth is about language; it is about what we as human moral agents say or express through our means of communication. This beginning recognizes that how we use our words is a significant and important moral endeavor. At a bare minimum, our speech presumes that what we say, in some sense, matches what is, and this is an inevitable aspect of communication. Everyone, for the most part, when he or she speaks, believes her or his words relate to, or express, what is actually the case. This is why "lying" is an accomplished art. One must presume others are telling the truth in order for the lie to work. If we thought lying was as basic to speaking as truth telling, we would never communicate.

"To say of what is . . ."

Truth is about language, but it is also more—it is also about "what is." Here is the difficulty. Do we have access to what is? Is there even such a thing as "what is"? If the Austrian economists are right, "what is" does not exist until our will imposes some value on it, but at the level of ordinary life, I think it is uncontroversial that we live and act as if there is something more to "what is." There are facts about human existence that are undeniable—we all must eat, take shelter from bad weather, live in some sort of community with others, depend on those others for our existence and for continued care. There are facts about historical events—Sophocles wrote *Oedipus Rex*. These facts assume minimal truth claims.

Other claims to "what is" are more difficult, claims such as there is a God, human beings are free, human beings have a moral purpose found in happiness, the beatific vision, or the greatest good for the greatest number. These are maximal truth claims. Telling the truth about the first set of claims, the minimal truth claims, is less controversial than to do so about the second; and making sure our language relates to, or expresses, reality is easier in the first than in the second. Yet, what makes us most human is attending to the maximal truth claims, even if discovering them is much more difficult than for the minimal truth claims. To abandon the maximal truth claims because they are difficult, and to speak only of the minimal truth claims because they are easily verifiable or falsifiable, is to abandon truth for data.

Truth, then, has two aspects. There is an unavoidable metaphysical aspect to truth. Metaphysics concerns first principles or the conditions that are taken to be the sufficient or necessary background for our ordinary actions. If there is no such thing as a meaningful existence, it would not make sense to ask how our words relate to it. Metaphysics examines difficult concepts such as being, essence, existence, and so on. Truth has a metaphysical aspect because it acknowledges "what is" as "what is." If there is nothing that *is*, there can be no truth telling. There is only value.

> Truth is possible because the world is God's good creation infused with an intelligibility that allows us to understand it.

Truth is possible not because the world is meaningless and only given meaning by our will. That way lies Trumpism and the devaluation of truth by power. Truth is possible because the world is God's good creation infused with an intelligibility that allows us to understand it, although that understanding requires effort. We do not gain this intelligibility through a violent grasping of things but through a peaceful enjoyment and joyous attentiveness.[1] The metaphysical aspect of truth makes

---

1   For an excellent theological account of creation, see Simon Oliver, *Creation: A Guide for the Perplexed* (London: Bloomsbury, 2017). For a joyous account of the life of a biologist seeking truth, see Hope Jahren's *Lab Girl* (New York: Knopf, 2017). She begins with a telling quote from

possible its moral aspect—the virtue of truth telling. If there is no truth in the world, there could be no virtue in speaking well about it. Yet if there is no virtue in speaking about it, we could not identify its metaphysical reality. The metaphysical and moral depend on each other. The only way to "what is" is through saying. Yet by speaking truthfully, we discover more fully that "what is" is.

"To say of what is that it is"

In Aristotle's definition, truth concerns language and "what is," but it goes beyond identifying the "what" to acknowledging "that" it is. The "what is" gives us knowledge of essences, ideas, or concepts. The "that it is" lets us know it actually exists; it is here and can be recognized, experienced, enjoyed. There is, then, a correlation between our language, the "what" it expresses, and the reality "that it is." Here is one of the main difficulties with truth; we seldom, if ever, have absolute certainty about that correlation. There are some simple examples of this correlation, some basic facts that are fairly uncontroversial. For instance, Sophocles wrote the play *Oedipus Rex*. If someone says Euripides wrote *Oedipus Rex*, we expect that when evidence is brought to their attention that this is not the case, they will change the way they speak. If someone says, "Who are you to hold me accountable? It is my right to say Euripides wrote *Oedipus Rex*," then we know that they are not interested in truth but only advantage and power. The virtue of truth telling requires a willingness to be accountable for our speech. When we make misstatements or what could be a lie, then faced with evidence, we should adjust our speech accordingly. Of course, with more difficult claims such as the old claim from the Westminster Shorter Catechism, "The chief end of the human being is to glorify God and enjoy him forever," things get much more difficult. We still expect people to be attentive to what they say and held accountable for it, but a

---

Helen Keller, "The more I handled things and learned their names and uses, the more joyous and confident grew my sense of kinship with the world."

resolution that we have spoken the truth—that our language matches reality—is more difficult.

The minimal truth claims are more easily resolved; the maximal ones are hardly resolvable at all. In either case, what we should recognize is that truth is not a single event. Truth is a virtuous activity that requires the cultivation of habits over time that assumes that I am careful and attentive in my use of language. I am willing to acknowledge and revise in the light of evidence. I can recognize reasonable alternative positions to my own, and I am open to giving and receiving counsel about them in a variety of communities—both those who agree with me and those who do not. In that sense, I think it is best to consider truth as a virtue—telling the truth.

> **The virtue of truth telling requires practice and a willingness to be accountable for our speech.**

As a virtue, truth telling is essential to politics for two reasons. First, political community of any sort, from the local bicycling club to the large bureaucratic nation-state or global corporation, cannot be sustained without a minimal account of truth telling. It is a necessary feature of human existence, and if it is denied, only deceit and coercive power hold us together, and that can never sustain us. Without truth, promises cannot be kept, correct information cannot be presented, plans cannot be made, and past mistakes cannot be rectified.

> **Political community of any sort cannot be sustained without truth telling.**

Second, politics as the good ordering of communities will also require attention to maximal truth claims, even if they are not easily attained. We should not expect the nation-state to decide on maximal truth claims, but it must allow for their pursuit even when that pursuit puts into question claims made by the nation-state. If we lose the quest for those goods, for maximal truth, we will become less human—and more like our computers and smartphones, which can take care of the minimal truths for us very well with a simple Google search.

While the metaphysics of truth is a necessary condition of our existence—something is or it is not—the virtue of truth telling is not. It is a practical activity of discovering, acknowledging, or making "what is" to be "that it is" through means of communication. It requires human agency. The virtues are not possessions we already have. We have dispositions for them, but those dispositions must be actualized. Virtues are habits that we can have if we properly exercise them, an exercise known as "habituation." The virtue of truth telling arises from the development of character in the context of a community of friends in which the virtue is necessary to sustain that community. Developing the virtue takes time, and we often fail. In her book *Putting on Virtue*, Jennifer Herdt, a Christian ethicist at Yale, argues that cultivating virtue assumes a "habituation gap."[2] The very activity of seeking to become what I am not yet acknowledges I am not yet what I should be. In that sense, virtue recognizes something I think most of us who seek to be ethical acknowledge—we are, in part, hypocrites. We are trying to be something we know we are not. We are trying to tell the truth when we are not always certain what that entails or if we have attained it. For virtue ethics, this poses little problem as long as we acknowledge it and remain accountable for our actions.

> **The virtue of truth telling arises from the development of character in the context of a community of friends in which the virtue is necessary to sustain that community.**

Let me give as an example as to how virtue works with the practice of teaching. Teaching requires preparatory research, putting together a course syllabus, contemplating how best to educate students—what to read, how to evaluate, etc. It assumes a habituation gap; students do not yet know everything that they need to know, or they would not need to be taught. Teaching is an activity that also has an end, a purpose; it aims at cultivating the virtues

---

2   Jennifer Herdt, *Putting on Virtue: The Legacy of the Splendid Vices* (Chicago, IL: University of Chicago Press, 2008), 23.

of wisdom, knowledge, and truth telling. These are the internal goods to the practice of teaching, and like all internal goods, they are noncompetitive. If one student gains wisdom, it does not take away from the possibility that others will as well. Internal goods assume external goods—taking attendance, giving grades, getting paid to teach or paying to learn, having a classroom, lights, and so on. The external goods are the condition for the internal goods, but they do not produce virtue.[3] Students can have perfect attendance and receive good grades and yet fail in achieving the virtue of wisdom, knowledge, or truth telling. For students to gain the virtues of wisdom, knowledge, and truth telling requires their self-involvement in the activity of learning that exceeds that of merely attending to the external goods. If they do not read, reflect, and engage with other students or teachers, those virtues cannot be attained.

One of the difficulties in every institution is that the external goods become more fundamental to its mission than the internal goods. The external goods may be important, but they are insufficient for virtue. Internal goods, like truth telling, are what matter most. The virtue of truth telling helps us identify something profoundly wrong with contemporary political life. It is dominated by practices that are external to any virtuous politics such as mass mobilization, unregulated financial contributions, misleading commercials, hired surrogates to provide favorable interpretations, voting, protests, and the assertion of rights. Some of these practices are external goods such as voting, protests, and asserting rights; others, such as hiring surrogates for spin, are not goods in any sense of the word. None of these practices assume that "telling the truth" is an internal good to the political life. They assume and propagate the idea that politics is about winning; politics involves defeating the opponent rather than deliberating about what is good for people.

Truth telling cannot be removed from politics or economics without negative consequences, which I tried to make clear in the

---

3   These distinctions come from Alasdair MacIntyre's *After Virtue: A Study in Moral Virtue* (Notre Dame, IN: University of Notre Dame Press, 2007).

first two chapters of this work. If political life is to be virtuous, then we must give an account of its internal goods; we must have an account of what political deliberation is for that is something more than winning. Here is the problem. If the virtue of truth telling is to be retrieved, we need a politics more concerned with deliberating over what is good for human beings than one concerned with winning, but such a politics is difficult because we have little agreement over what is good for human beings. As Robin Lovin notes, "Modern politics cannot be Aristotelian, because the requirements of order dictate a justice that is not tied to questions about the good."[4] Large, modern democratic nation-states are about order and security, not truth and goodness. They work only on the basis of the thinnest account of truth and goodness possible with the hope that smaller, voluntary associations will pursue their thicker account of what is true and good within the order and security the modern nation-state makes possible. The state's role is to manage the conflict so that the smaller, voluntary associations do not war with each other. For this reason, political life within the modern nation-state is often described as "civil war by other means." The difficulty with this analysis is that it did not, and very well may not, prevent "civil war by other means" from becoming civil war by means of civil war.

I agree with Lovin's analysis in part. Like him, I have no desire to see the leaders of nation-states make judgments about what is true or good and impose them on us through force. At most, we expect the minimal account of truth telling from our politicians,

> If the virtue of truth telling is to be retrieved, we need a politics more concerned with deliberating over what is good for human beings than one concerned with winning, but such a politics is difficult because we have little agreement over what is good for human beings.

---

4   Robin Lovin, *Christian Realism and the New Realities* (Cambridge: Cambridge University Press, 2008), 61.

and even then, we are not surprised that it happens so seldom, but because we have such a thin account of what the good is that politics should serve, the modern state can only be post-political. Whether it truly sustains an order within which voluntary associations can pursue their individual goods is also an open question.

Stanley Hauerwas expresses skepticism about the modern, liberal state's capacity to sustain the pursuits of voluntary associations. He has noted that "liberalism," by which he means the bureaucratic, modern nation-state, is "not simply a theory of government but a theory of society that is imperial in its demands." He continues: "I certainly believe there is much right about our [liberal] social order. Moreover, I think that liberalism has, sometimes almost in spite of itself, had some beneficial results. It is still unclear if some of those results, such as freedom of religion, can be sustained in a consistently worked out liberal society. For liberalism has been successful partly because it could depend on social structures and habits it did not create and in fact over time undermines."[5] One such habit is the virtue of truth telling, a virtue found in a diversity of communities and one sorely needed if liberalism is not to be "consistently worked out." Perhaps what we see with Trumpism is a consistently worked-out liberalism. Truth no longer matters because, as Trump has explicitly said again and again, all that matters is winning.

One way to retrieve the virtue of truth telling will require a twofold path. The first is a thicker account of what politics is for than liberalism allows. The second is the witness of the church as a transnational community that would both affirm this natural account of politics and stand as a constant reminder that there is no politics of perfection in this world to which we owe final allegiance.

Natural Human Flourishing

Although I shall argue below for the importance of the church maintaining its distance from the state's power in order to provide

---

5   Stanley Hauerwas, *Against the Nations: War and Survival in a Liberal Society* (Notre Dame, IN: University of Notre Dame Press, 1992), 18.

a witness to something more than natural, to the Great City for which we wait in patience, it is never sufficient, advisable, or possible for the church to hunker down in some enclave immune from all those peoples and communities who are not part of the church. Some have suggested that we must hunker down until we get another St. Benedict, which has become known as the "Benedict option." While we always hope for saints who show us the way forward, waiting for them never means withdrawing from the earthly cities that provide so many goods for us. Rather than the Benedict option, we need to be always mindful of St. Augustine's insistence that Christians live in two cities—the earthly city and the city of God. The church is the first fruits of the city of God, but no one can live only in the church. It does not deliver mail, remove garbage, provide all necessary health care, educate everyone, offer safe shelter, and so on. It can, and does, of course, participate in many of these activities, but it does so in cooperation with others. Christians always act in both cities, the city of God and the earthly city. We have something to say about the natural goods necessary for the flourishing of all God's creatures. To explain this requires we return briefly to the previous discussion of liberty.

Recall that what constitutes freedom is contested. While everyone should seek freedom, there is little agreement on what it is. Following Isaiah Berlin's famous 1958 essay, I suggested that freedom is divided between negative and positive freedom. Negative liberty was divided between two poles, liberal and republican. Liberal freedom is noninterference. We are free insofar as our agency can effect its will in the world without unnecessary interference from others. There are two poles in this understanding of freedom: libertarian or liberal egalitarian. The former would be the disciples of Friedrich Hayek or even Ayn Rand; the latter would be those of John Stuart Mill or John Rawls. Their difference is the extent to which government plays a role in regulating noninterference.

Government has a role in both poles of liberal freedom, which is why both libertarians and liberal egalitarians seek public office. For libertarians, government's role is primarily negative; it is to enforce voluntary contracts, preserve property rights, ensure equality of opportunity, and punish those who would violate contract and property rights. It is to establish security and order so that corporations and other voluntary associations can pursue what they pursue with little to no interference. Liberal egalitarians have more of a role for government; its purpose, in their view, also includes enforcing contracts and preserving property rights, but it goes beyond this by also supporting government efforts to ensure not only equality of opportunity but conditions that would diminish inequality—so it would include something like the German codetermination model for corporate governance in which a certain percentage of corporate boards should be composed of workers or Elizabeth Warren's "Accountable Capitalism Act."[6]

Republican freedom is also a form of negative freedom, but rather than noninterference, it is freedom from domination. We are free insofar as we cannot be dominated by others, either a minority dominated by a majority or a majority dominated by a minority. Republican freedom requires government involvement in policies of "reconstruction" to address historic wrongs, acknowledging them and seeking to repair them. Republican freedom was attempted during Reconstruction but has not been a dominant form of freedom in the US. The civil rights movement, and especially Dr. King's "Economic Bill of Rights," could be seen as a republican view of freedom. But in truth, most of our political and economic policies occur in the space between a libertarian view of freedom (which somehow gets named conservativism) and a liberal egalitarian view of freedom (which somehow gets named "the Left").

Each of these accounts of freedom differs in the "thickness" of the accounts of truth and goodness necessary for them. The thinnest is the libertarian. I fear, as I noted in chapter 2, that it leads to nihilism. It led to Trumpism, and that is a historical fact. Liberal egalitarianism has a bit thicker account. It would require more attention to the virtue of justice, and truth is always a matter

---

6   For a discussion of the latter, see Christine Emba's "Elizabeth Warren Is Giving Capitalism the Moral Rehab It Needs," *Washington Post*, August 30, 2018.

of justice.[7] Recovering the political option of a genuine republican freedom would be a marked improvement over our current state of affairs, but none of these accounts of freedom offers a sufficiently dense account of what politics is for, and here we need to turn away from a negative liberty to the positive liberty intrinsic to the virtue tradition.

The positive liberty that I am advocating has both a natural and a theological component. Alasdair MacIntyre's work on human flourishing sets forth well the natural end that politics and economics should support. In contrast to long-standing moral and political traditions that claim such a natural end is too controversial, he suggests the following eight goods that are independent of any single culture:

(1) good health,
(2) a standard of living free from destitution (food, clothing, shelter),
(3) good family relationships,
(4) sufficient education that allows one to develop her or his powers,
(5) productive and rewarding work,
(6) good friends,
(7) leisure activities beyond work, and
(8) "the ability of a rational agent to order one's life and to identify and learn from one's mistakes."[8]

Something like these eight points would provide the good that politics and economics should serve. The virtue of truth telling would then have a role in politics because we would have to ask if our policies and practices were achieving these goods. We would have a common standard by which we could evaluate well our use of language in deliberating about what is good. This account of

---

7 For an account of society based on liberal egalitarianism that would attend to truth telling and justice more so than libertarianism, see Tommie Shelby's *Dark Ghettos: Injustice, Dissent, and Reform* (Cambridge, MA: Belknap Press of Harvard University Press, 2016).

8 Alasdair MacIntyre, *Ethics in the Conflict of Modernity* (Cambridge: Cambridge University Press, 2016), 222.

the goods that politics should serve is much thicker than what a libertarian, liberal-egalitarian, or republican freedom offers, but without something like them, retrieving the virtue of truth telling will be highly unlikely. We are left with an adversarial politics of power and advantage.

The truth will not set us free if the only way we have to be political is through the post-political reality of the large, modern, bureaucratic nation-state and its negative freedoms. The truths that will set us free require deliberations about the good that we hold in common with all creatures. It is unclear to me that we can expect the politics of the nation-state to begin such a deliberation. There are too many entrenched powers whose interests have no stake in that conversation. Presidents, senators, and national representatives will not lead that conversation. It begins in neighborhoods, villages, cities, states. If it begins there, perhaps it can "trickle up" to the national level, but we need not hold our breath or expect it to do so before we set about the task of ordering our neighborhoods, villages, cities, and states to these eight goods. They must be part of our political and economic conversations.

> The truth that will set us free requires personal and intentional deliberation about the goods we hold in common with all creatures.

As a theologian, I would go a step further than MacIntyre and argue that freedom is found when one's life is ordered not only toward the good but also toward God, who is the source of goodness. Let me quote a line from the prayer of confession from the United Methodist Church's Eucharistic service to illustrate an account of positive freedom. After confessing that we have not loved God as we should, nor our neighbor, that we broke God's law and did not hear the cry of the needy, we pray: "Free us for joyful obedience." We are free when we are free for God. As St. Augustine noted, the will is unfree if it follows its own desires without any graced direction; then it is "*incurvatus se*," turned in upon itself. It is free when it is

> Freedom is found in God, who is the source of goodness.

directed toward the love of God and neighbor by being moved outside itself. *It is not and never should be the role of the modern nation-state to enforce this positive freedom.* The church sets forth this fuller positive freedom by being a "light" that attracts and never a power that dominates. Seeking state power to enforce the church's account of the good has also brought us to Trumpism.

The Ecclesial Approach

A crucial question for the retrieval of the virtue of truth telling is, Who is the "we" that should do something? There is no single answer to that question. In fact, there are multiple "we's" who foster and sustain the virtue of truth telling: families, diverse nations, voluntary associations, universities—all have their part to play. But I would like to conclude this work by focusing on the "we" who is the church. We contributed to the rise of Trumpism. We are obligated to address it, and that will require thinking of the church as more than a voluntary religious association within civil society whose purpose is to legitimate a national identity.

Many place the church within civil society as one voluntary association among others. To accept that placement, however, is to subordinate the church to the state, something that would repeat the second difficulty we face that was noted in the five hypotheses of chapter 3; the church becomes reduced to a nationalist project dependent upon the state. No one with an adequate doctrine of the church as the Body of Christ should accept this subordination. As John Coleman has stated: "Most Christian theorists—at least with anything approaching a somewhat robust ecclesiology (i.e., the doctrine of the Church)—see the Church as also somehow apart from the other free associations of civil society. Its authority derives from God and not from the state or the associational nexus of civil society. The Church is *in* but not really fully *of* civil society."[9] The church is a transnational reality that cannot and

---

9   John A. Coleman, S.J., "A Limited State and a Vibrant Society: Christianity and Civil Society," in *Civil Society and Government*, ed. Nancy L. Rosenblum and Robert C. Post (Princeton, NJ: Princeton University

should not be confined by state boundaries. In that sense, it must make itself an exception to state laws that seek to limit the pursuit of the good to those boundaries.

The church should have something to say about the relationship between the state and the nations that constitute the modern state, and I made an attempt to set that forth in the previous section by advocating for a thicker account of the good that politics should serve. Yet as was argued in chapter 1, especially with the discussion of Hebrews and its depiction of Jesus as our priest-king, the church is itself something like a nation. Those who belong to it are repeatedly referred to in Scripture as "citizens" of a different kind of politics. This citizenship is not an otherworldly citizenship but one that begins now through Christ's odd victory in his cross and resurrection. His odd victory creates a people who look to him as the purpose for a faithful politics that will require a fuller notion of its goods than MacIntyre suggests. It will include the infused virtues of faith, hope, and charity that require subjecting unjust laws to rigorous interrogation. Ample evidence for these virtues and their political significance could be provided in Scripture and tradition. We could speak about Dr. King's witness to these virtues in his "Letter from a Birmingham Jail," and his prophetic reminder, drawing on St. Augustine and Thomas Aquinas, that an unjust law is no law at all, but let me provide examples from two Methodist bishops that show us the kind of leadership we need if we are to be a church who tells the truth.

In 1850 the institution of slavery in the US took on a new and even yet more vicious reality. As a capitulation to slaveholding states, the US Congress passed the Fugitive Slave Act, which allowed slave owners to track down escaped slaves everywhere, including in nonslaveholding states, and return them as property to their "rightful" owners. This act had the support of law. The Methodist bishop Gilbert Haven spoke out against the Fugitive Slave Act, stating, "In Christ, not in the Constitution, must we put

---

Press, 2002), 225. I discuss this more fully in *Augustinian and Ecclesial Christian Ethics: On Loving Enemies* (Lanham, MD: Fortress Academic Press, 2017).

our trust." He understood that the church is not founded upon the US Constitution or any act of the will. It is founded upon Christ, and it must be obedient to him. He is the good to which Christians' freedom must be ordered.

Likewise, Bishop J. W. Loguen of the African Methodist Episcopal Zion Church challenged the Fugitive Slave Act by calling local cities to practice civil disobedience, calling "the city of Syracuse to defy the laws of the land and declare itself a city of refuge."[10] A local city can enact this freedom by making itself a sanctuary for the most vulnerable and defying an unjust law.

These two bishops exercised faithful oversight of the church. Contrast that with the recent ruling by a United Methodist superintendent against the charges brought against the United Methodist layperson Jeff Sessions for separating children from parents and placing them in cages. More than six hundred United Methodist clergy and laity accused him of violating the United Methodist Church's *Discipline* against abusing children. The charges were brought before his superintendent, and she made the following ruling:

> A political action is not personal conduct when the political officer is carrying out official policy. In this matter, Attorney General Jeff Sessions was carrying out the official policy of the President and/or the United States Department of Justice. It was not an individual act. I believe this type of conduct is not covered by the chargeable offense provisions of *The Book of Discipline* of The United Methodist Church, 2016 for laypersons. Therefore, your complaint is dismissed.

This is a failure of faithful leadership and a rejection of Christian freedom. It subordinates the Christian's positive freedom to the negative freedom of the modern nation-state. If abolitionists had this sentiment, we would have never had the witness of Bishops Haven and Loguen. The church must have something more to say than this. Let me give an example of how it can do this by discussing

10 Ted A. Smith, *Weird John Brown: Divine Violence and the Limits of Ethics* (Stanford, CA: Stanford University Press, 2015), 94–95.

the Supreme Court decision *Citizens United*, a failure on the part of the Supreme Court to encourage the virtue of truth telling.

Money, Truth, and Political Speech

In 2010 the US Supreme Court ruled by a 5 to 4 decision that limitations on corporate donations to political campaigns violated the First Amendment. Such limitations were tantamount to restricting free speech. The corporation, which is considered a "person" in US law, was granted the freedom to speak, and financial contributions were considered speech. One result of this 2010 decision was that the "speech" corporations uttered could remain anonymous. In July 2012 two Republican senators, Warren Rudman and Chuck Hagel, wrote an op-ed in the *New York Times* warning not only about the increased contributions in the 2012 elections coming from "extremely wealthy individuals, corporations and trade unions" but also about the anonymity by which such "persons" were allowed to speak:

> Yet what really alarms us about this situation is that we can't find out who is behind these blatant attempts to control the outcome of our elections. We are inundated with extraordinarily negative advertising on television every evening and have no way to know who is paying for it and what their agenda might be. In fact, it's conceivable that we have created such a glaring loophole in our election process that foreign interests could directly influence the outcome of our elections. And we might not even know it had happened until after the election, if at all.[11]

Rudman and Hagel make an important and interesting point. Given what we know about the 2016 election, their 2012 words were prescient. They speak from the perspective of US senators concerned about the integrity of the democratic process.

---

11 Warren Rudman and Chuck Hagel, "For Political Closure, We Need Disclosure," *New York Times*, July 16, 2012, http://campaignstops.blogs.nytimes.com/2012/07/16/for-political-closure-we-need-disclosure/?ref=federalelectioncommission.

Rudman and Hagel identify the problem as the lack of transparency by and accountability for the "persons" who are speaking to us in political campaigns in and through corporations. They suggest this could lead to "foreign interests" dominating US politics. Christian theology should both question and affirm their identification of the problem. It should question if the primary issue is "foreign interests" dominating US politics. Christians have obligations that extend beyond the nation's boundaries. As Dr. Martin Luther King Jr. once put it: "We are made to live together because of the interrelated network of mutuality, tied into a single garment of destiny. Whatever affects one directly, affects all indirectly."[12] Christians must consult all the baptized along with all people of goodwill in foreign lands about how our national policies affect them. We need this kind of interference in our elections. Because US policies have global reach, members of the Christian church in the US should listen to those outside the US who are affected by its policies and make sure their interests are represented in any good, free, transparent, political discussion.

We have obligations that exceed that of "America First." Take as an example the much-discussed caravan of people from Honduras making their way to the US to seek asylum. Rather than consult the politicians or their pundits, we should be asking laypersons, pastors, and bishops in Honduras what the reality is. What is going on in Honduras, and why are so many fleeing? As the baptized, we have obligations to those seeking refuge; Jesus has told us that welcoming them is welcoming him. United Methodists could gather a council of people from both places in order to ask about the facts and then decide how to respond. United Methodists could open their homes to those seeking asylum, and the same could be true of every church. It would be a much better way to engage our neighbors politically than the expensive, and primarily symbolic, deployment of troops to the southern border.

---

12 See Martin Luther King Jr., "Letter from a Birmingham Jail," https://www.africa.upenn.edu/Articles_Gen/Letter_Birmingham.html.

Rudman and Hagel's concern, however, is not primarily with this kind of "foreign interest" but with the large anonymous contributions any corporation can now make in US politics. They do not identify the problem as free speech per se. All sides would agree, I believe, that free speech should be affirmed. Although the Roman Catholic Church once held that "error has no rights," no church today, including Roman Catholicism, still upholds the curtailment of speech. But why do the churches and others affirm free speech? As we saw above, the affirmation of free speech is also found among white nationalists who want to weaponize it and broaden the domain of what is acceptable for discussion so that their heinous views become mainstream. D. W. Griffiths did that in 1915; Richard Spencer attempts it today.

Free speech at its best allows for the broadest possible discernment so that truth will not be a mere function of power. If speech does not serve truth, it serves only the interest of power.

Free speech at its best allows for the broadest possible discernment in order that truth will not be a mere function of power. If speech does not serve truth, it serves only the interest of power. Speech in service to hate leads to violence and massacres. Speech in service to power will not make anyone free. It leads to despotism, not politics. Yet censoring speech through the state's control of the means of violence is seldom liberatory. We face a dilemma. The virtue of truth telling requires a disciplined use of speech in service to what is true or good. The nation-state is the primary institution that has the power to hold speech accountable to truth, but it is the least equipped to execute that power, especially when it has become defined by contending interests rather than truth. Other associations or disciplines must exercise the virtue of truth telling without tying it to the coercion of state power. Journalism, the universities, and the church must fulfill this role. The serious problem Rudman and Hagel identify, which Christian theology should affirm and explore, is, What constitutes a person who can speak freely, and how can persons be held accountable for their speech?

In order to gain clarity, and possibly an answer, to the question Hagel and Rudman identified, the Christian Church should, from the perspective of its faith and teachings, affirm the following three points:

1. The purpose of politics is to serve the good of persons and not vice versa.
2. Persons, not corporations, are creatures made in the image of God.
3. For politics to serve the good of persons, speech must not only be free but also accountable. Unless we adopt a thoroughgoing libertarian freedom, freedom cannot be freedom without accountability. Accountability presumes truth.

Let me take up each of these points in turn.

The Purpose of Politics Is to Serve the Good of Persons and Not Vice Versa

The state does not serve God by establishing a church and giving it privileges in return for its submission and service. Nor is the state a salvific institution that will continue once the Kingdom arrives. Like marriage, it has a purpose limited to the time between the times, the times between Christ's First and Second Coming. It serves God inasmuch as it accepts those limited purposes— encourage good, restrain evil, and preserve social cohesion. Its policies should serve these ends. They are ends that assist the church in fulfilling its mission of worship and witness and help God's creatures flourish.

Of course, what constitutes "good," "evil," and "social cohesion" is contested as we saw above in the crash course on political theory. There are some things about which everyone should agree with little challenge. Concentration camps, genocide, and ethnic cleansing are evils that destroy social cohesion and do not contribute to the good. I think (or once thought) that we would agree that separating children from their parents and placing them in cages was so despicable that it would be unthinkable. It, too, destroys social cohesion and should not be, should not have been, tolerated. There are others about which people of goodwill disagree. Free speech can provide conditions to negotiate those disagreements. Its purpose should be to serve the common good through a peaceful exchange of ideas committed to seeking the truth about what is good. Civility is not a matter of politeness, decorum, or deference. Duels were very polite events. Civility concerns a willingness to speak the truth by giving and receiving counsel in a context of nonviolence that is then willing to be accountable for what one has said. Lying and bullshitting are at the core of incivility. When lying and bullshitting rule the day, there may be no option but to start shouting. Loud or offensive speech is not necessarily false; it can express the truth better than calm, sedate, yet deceitful speech. Sometimes temples need to be cleansed.

Christianity also recognizes the difficulty in the search for truth and goodness because of sin. As St. Augustine put it, the fundamental political problem for any truly just society is that our relations are often more constituted by deceit than truth. "The lie" is the fundamental problem of sin in Augustine. It too often constitutes political society as well as many of our social relations.[13] What can save us from the lie? Robert Dodaro provides an Augustinian answer: "Augustine argues that human beings are united to Christ when they accept in faith and humility that virtue derives from the mediation of Christ's grace. Thus, united in Christ as members of his body, these believers form the just society."[14]

> Anyone incapable of acknowledging fault cannot be just.

Christ's redemption should restore truth first to the community found in his name and through it to all creation. The reason for this is simple. It is not because of the moral superiority of the

---

13 Robert Dodaro, *Christ and the Just Society in the Thought of Augustine* (Cambridge: Cambridge University Press, 2004), 69.

14 Dodaro, *Christ and the Just Society in the Thought of Augustine*, 71.

church, but because it was founded upon faith and humility rather than desire for glory. In order to have a political society founded upon truth, faith and humility rather than glory and power must be its basis; for faith and humility make possible an essential condition for truth telling: a political society that would be "truly penitential" and capable of acknowledging the truth of its sinful past.[15]

It can remember without deceit. Anyone incapable of acknowledging fault could not be just. For Augustine, "only those leaders whose church encourages them to acknowledge their sins and to seek pardon from God can hope to avoid the desire to dominate others."[16] In order to acknowledge our sin, our speech must not only be free but also accountable. We must know the truth about ourselves and be willing not only to acknowledge it but also to be held accountable for it. Which brings us to the second and third points: What constitutes a person capable of free speech who can pursue the limited ends of politics?

> **A just political society must be founded upon truth, faith, and humility rather than glory and power.**

Persons, Not Corporations, Are Creatures Made in the Image of God

When the US Supreme Court ruled that corporations are persons whose speech cannot be regulated, it did not intend to give political contests over to the highest bidder. Despite their good intentions, however, the Supreme Court ruling raises two issues that the Christian church should have addressed but has not. First, what constitutes a "person"? Second, what constitutes "speech"?

What constitutes a person? Boethius, a sixth-century philosopher, gave the classic definition of a "person": "A person is an individual substance of a rational nature." By an "individual," he meant that a person could not be divided into further parts. By substance, he meant that a person had an integrity; he or she was not merely contingent like the color of hair or skin. For Boethius,

---

15 Dodaro, *Christ and the Just Society in the Thought of Augustine*, 112.
16 Dodaro, *Christ and the Just Society in the Thought of Augustine*, 202.

the person's integrity is characterized by the ability to reason; a person has a rational nature. Boethius's definition became a standard answer to the question of what it means to be made in the "image of God" (Genesis 1:26).

Humankind is made in the "image of God," but exactly what that means is not specified in the Bible. Because God is depicted in Holy Scripture as a rational, personal acting subject, the human creature as made in God's image became associated with an analogous understanding of subjectivity. Like many aspects of Christian tradition, this traditional depiction of the "image of God" has been debated, and for good reason; it raises some important questions. What does the definition mean for human creatures who never had, or will lose, their rational capacity? Will they still be considered human? Should we even give a definition to what it means to be a human person? If we do, will it give a pretext to some in authority to exclude and exterminate those who do not fit the definition? We have too many historical examples of such exclusion to neglect these important questions, but now that the corporation has been defined as a "person," some such definition is important. Moreover, we should not forget that it is Nietzsche and the Austrian school of economics who rejected setting forth any universal, natural condition for human flourishing, something that thinkers as different as Aristotle, Aquinas, and Marx thought was essential to be truly human.[17]

Although it should not be used to exclude human creatures from proper protections, the definition of the person in Christian tradition means at least this: To be created in the image of God is to be a free, rational acting subject located in a nexus of relationships within God's good creation that requires certain goods for human flourishing. As a free rational agent, persons and their communities can be held accountable for their actions. This understanding of the acting subject differentiates human persons from other forms of subjects such as hurricanes or earthquakes. We do

---

17 For Nietzsche and the Austrian school's rejection, see Corey Robin, *The Reactionary Mind: Conservatism from Edmund Burke to Donald Trump*, 2nd ed. (Oxford: Oxford University Press, 2018), 151.

not hold them accountable for their actions because they are not individual subjects of a rational nature. This normative definition of human personhood does not rule out exceptions. Some human persons cannot be held accountable for their actions but are still considered human; it is an exception enshrined in law. But the exception proves the norm. When people speak and act, they are considered integral agents who can be held accountable for such speech and action. Without this accountability, core practices of the Christian tradition would make no sense—baptism, conversion, confirmation, marriage, ordination, and much more. These practices can be performed on persons. No corporation can be baptized, converted, married, or ordained. It is not a person. It has no individual, rational nature because it cannot tell us the truth by making a confession or vow and be held accountable. This is especially true of the limited liability company.

What is speech? Human speech is intrinsic to human persons. Such a definition does not reject that nonhuman creatures have a type of speech. The biological evidence for communication among other creatures is too compelling to neglect, but the speech that constitutes political society is an intentional action that only human persons perform. It occurs in diverse ways—orally, writing, gestures, and multiple forms of making signs. The exchange of money is a sign that communicates. It can be a form of speech when it is an intentional action performed by a human person who is capable of being accountable for it. Baking a cake could be a form of speech, and no one should be forced to say things he or she does not intend to say. Refusing to bake a cake is also a form of speech. In both cases, the intentional expression should be accountable to one's neighbors by examining what it communicates.

For Politics to Serve the Good of Persons, Speech Must Not Only Be Free but Also Accountable

Not only core practices of the Christian tradition but also those of politics make little to no sense if we fail to acknowledge persons as free, rational agents who can be held accountable for their actions, including their speech. To do so, the source of the speech and action must be able to be identified. If I speak or act and then deny I was its source, the result is deceit rather than truth. Apart from exceptional cases, we call that "lying."

The only way for truth to be served, and thus for the possibility of a just political society, is for persons to be held accountable for their speaking and acting. Such accountability is missing when the corporation is considered an anonymous person whose donations are considered speech. The corporation is not an "individual" who has an integrity that can be identified. Corporations can be broken down into their constituent parts: CEOs, boards of directors, other administrators, workers, and shareholders. Each of them can be persons who are held responsible for their actions, but the corporation itself is not an acting person in any traditional sense. It cannot really be identified. As Robert Palmiter puts it in his textbook on corporate law: "The corporation is a creature of law—a legal artifice. Nobody has ever seen one."[18] It is not a person who can be identified and held accountable, and therefore on Christian grounds, it cannot be a person. It is a fiction. Perhaps such a fiction has its use in law, but such uses are what should concern us.

Most corporations are "persons" with limited liability. They can speak through unlimited donations but with limited accountability. Although Christians should not reject the corporation itself, they should be suspicious about the purpose served by a fictional person called the corporation, who can speak and act without accountability.[19] Whether readers find such suspicions warranted, they should at least recognize the profound difficulties that having such political actors creates for a truthful and just society and contribute their own resources to solving the problems identified by Rudman and Hagel. If we are to have the virtue of truth telling, the insidious effects of *Citizens United* will need to be corrected.

---

18 Robert Palmiter, *Corporations: Examples & Explanations*, 4th ed. (New York: Aspen, 2003), 3.

19 For a sobering discussion of some negative consequences of this fiction, see Lawrence E. Mitchell, *Corporate Irresponsibility: America's Newest Export* (New Haven, CT: Yale University Press, 2001).

Conclusion

Where do we go from here?

1. The *first* thing we should do is change the discussion of the "we" who should do something. Too much of our political, ethical, and cultural discussion assumes that the agents of history, the true subjects that matter, are national politicians, warriors, or wealthy businesspersons. Despite the suspicion that Holy Scripture casts on these characters, they have been shown partiality in contemporary life by being elected to office, appointed to high political office, designated as members of boards overseeing nearly every aspect of life from business to the university, and constantly rewarded and celebrated. The celebration of such characters reveals how power has become more significant than truth. Government and commerce become the exclusive focus of our ethics and the preoccupation of our cultural and social life. Even when we consider other aspects of life such as the place of the church or universities, the role of artists, journalists, and other professions, they are placed within this dominating context. The context for political discourse needs to be broadened.

> **Broaden the context for political discourse to include caregivers.**

One way to broaden the context could be through a feminist ethics of care. Rather than considering the politician, warrior, or wealthy businessperson as the paradigmatic agent, we should think of caregivers as those agents. The central question, then, is not about war or commerce, but who cared for you and for whom do you care, and how do we sustain the conditions that allow care to flourish? Virginia Held identifies five characteristics for such an ethics of care: "First, the central focus of the ethics of care is on the compelling moral salience of attending to and meeting the needs of the particular others for whom we take responsibility." We all had our diapers changed at the beginning of life. Many of us engaged in changing diapers during the course of our life, and most of us will need the same kind of care at the end of our life. Changing diapers is just a symbol for care, but it is an important one. Anyone who has lived his or her life without ever having to change a diaper should be placed under suspicion. Politicians and CEOs should be asked when they last changed one. If they have not, they should not be entrusted with power.

Second, such an ethics values emotion as well as reason. It does not set them against each other, seeking a cold, calculating rationality. Narratives that emerge from in-depth relationships, such as those found around kitchen tables, are more important than mining data on the internet.

Third, it rejects "impartiality." We are not to be impartial observers who make decisions from a "veil of ignorance," but our partiality toward those for whom we care and who care for us has ethical and cultural significance. We should seek their flourishing.

Fourth, it "reconceptualizes" what is considered "public" and what is "private." Some of this has already occurred in our culture with powerful movements such as #MeToo. Sexual abuse is no longer considered a private matter. Marital rape, once thought impossible and beyond the law, is now recognized as possible and criminal. Positively caring for others through daily life should be considered to serve the common good more than what the politician, warrior, or wealthy businessperson accomplishes. What would it mean to say to women and men who have taken on the arduous duty of caring for children, the elderly, or those incapable of caring for themselves, "Thank you for your service"?

I once taught a course titled "Violence, Forgiveness, and Reconciliation" at a Jesuit university. The course met throughout the semester and concluded by taking primarily Catholic students to stay with Protestant households in Northern Ireland for two weeks and observe ecumenical works to build peace. The course was taught both before and after the Easter Day Accords, the truce between Catholics and Protestants. On one occasion, we visited a Catholic-Protestant daycare on the Falls Road. We asked the women how they came together in the midst of the troubles and were told, "Babies still need to be cared for; their diapers changed." Changing diapers could be a condition necessary for peace just as some peace is required to change diapers. Finally, a feminist ethics of care has a unique conception of the person, eschewing both the rational, autonomous agent of Kantianism, who is primarily a citizen of the nation-state, and the self-interested agent of utilitarianism, who is primarily a citizen of the market. Instead, the person is conceived as an agent who will always be a giver or recipient of care. Thus, the person is intrinsically relational and an encumbered self.[20]

2. If we are to sustain conditions that make for truth telling, something must be done to address income inequality. Income inequality is not only an injustice-generating vice, but it is also politically destabilizing. Gross conditions of inequality eventually lead to civil unrest. The US has been ruled by an ideology at least since the "Washington Consensus" that inequalities in wealth serve the alleviation of poverty. In turn, the wealthy business owner has become the entitled agent to whom many look for leadership. What Trumpism resolutely demonstrates is that wisdom, truth, and wealth bear little to no relation to each other. It is time to remember the words of Jesus, "It is easier for a camel to go through an eye of a needle than for someone who is rich to enter the Kingdom of Heaven" (Matthew 19:24). Of course, even this is possible for God, but the benefit of the doubt should go not to those of us with wealth but to those without it.

Such a statement should not valorize involuntary poverty, nor does it teach that everyone must give everything away, take a vow of poverty, and join a community of goods (although some have and that should be honored). Jesus himself lived from the surplus of others (Luke 8:3). He did not work, did not find his or others' dignity in work, but was free from work for mission. He called his

---

20 Virginia Held, *The Ethics of Care: Personal, Political, and Global* (Oxford: Oxford University Press, 2006), 10–14, 47. I am grateful to, and have been influenced by, Eric Gregory's work. He showed me how the ecclesial approach to ethics could learn from and make common cause with a feminist ethics of care (see Eric Gregory, *Politics and the Order of Love: An Augustinian Ethics of Democratic Citizenship* [Chicago, IL: University of Chicago Press, 2008], 164–73). I discuss this in *Augustinian and Ecclesial Christian Ethics* (Lanham, MD: Fortress Academic Press, 2018), 199–200.

disciples away from work. Dignity arises from God's creating activity and not work, especially degrading conditions of work under which many people continue to labor. We must start telling the truth about work, and in so doing address its inequalities. God did not create some persons to serve others by cleaning their toilets or working in miserable conditions. If our freedom arises from others' toil, then bondage conditions freedom, and that cannot be true freedom.

Matthew Bruenig offers some concrete suggestions for how we can address income inequality. For him, "socialism" should cease being a word that causes people to rage in apoplectic fits, and instead we should consider some viable means for implementing a healthier, democratic spirit, such as strengthening labor markets and increasing public ownership of capital. The latter could be accomplished through a "social wealth fund" filled "with capital assets purchased on the open market." He also advocates that the government should "build at least 10 million units of publicly owned, mixed-income social housing, which would both increase public ownership of the US housing stock and provide a much-needed boost to the housing supply in prohibitively expensive metropolitan areas."[21]

I find Matt Bruenig's work full of promise. I am insufficiently skilled in economics to know its limits, but I am sufficiently aware of politics to know that we seldom have interesting discussions about such policies because anything that questions the dominant ideology privileging the wealthy is shouted down. Notice he does not advocate a corps of jackbooted socialist guards who kick down doors and claim all property for the revolution. If we are to have a conversation grounded in truth and reason rather than power, then alternatives like the ones Bruenig suggests

---

21 Charles Krupa, "What Would a Socialist America Look Like?," *Politico Magazine*, September 3, 2018, https://www.politico.com/magazine/story/2018/09/03/what-would-a-socialist-america-look-like-219626. See also Matt Bruenig, "Nickel-and-Dime Socialism," Medium, February 11, 2017, https://medium.com/@MattBruenig/nickel-and-dime-socialism-47fcec 406295.

should be granted a hearing. I doubt that will happen in any state-led political discourse for the foreseeable future. Both political parties have a stake in business as usual. Electing and appointing billionaire businessmen reaffirms those stakes. Billionaire businessmen appointing and electing politicians does so as well.

For proposals such as Bruenig's to gain a hearing, we also need to challenge the dominance of wealth over our lives. One place to begin is A. Q. Smith's essay titled "It's Basically Just Immoral to Be Rich," in which he wrote, "Here is a simple statement of principle that doesn't get repeated enough: if you possess billions of dollars, in a world where many people struggle because they do not have much money, you are an *immoral* person."[22] Anyone who has read Holy Scripture knows that Smith and Jesus are on the same page. He goes on to note that white families in the US have sixteen times the wealth as black families. How is that justifiable? Of course, there are economists, think tanks, politicians, and even theologians who will justify it, but in the end reasonable people, and especially reasonable people of faith, should know there is little truth in such justifications.

Smith's essay avoids some vexing questions. He does not advocate for socialism. He does not side with capitalists against socialists or socialists against capitalists. He does not address the structural issues that social justice advocates frequently address. He appeals to charity, to giving away our excess to make the lives of others bearable. He knows that for some reason many people today on both the left and the right reject appeals to charity. We have all heard the tired phrase, "If you give someone a fish, they eat for a day, but if you teach them how to fish, they eat for a lifetime." Having lived in a fishing village in Honduras, I'm not convinced that teaching people to fish gets them out of poverty.

---

22 A. Q. Smith, "It's Basically Just Immoral to Be Rich," *Current Affairs*, June 14, 2017, https://www.currentaffairs.org/2017/06/its-basically-just -immoral-to-be-rich.

Smith does not make an economic argument; he makes a moral one. He avoids the question of how we earn our income and addresses something that should be recognizable, especially to anyone in the Wesleyan tradition, as a key aspect of faith—how much of it you keep. Even if we somehow deserved earning one hundred, one thousand, ten thousand times more than our neighbor, are we justified in keeping it? He says no and advocates moral shaming for those who do; something we know none of our current political parties would dare attempt. He suggests a simple, nonradical proposal. We develop a moral culture where we establish a "maximum moral income"; anyone who keeps over $250,000 annual income for a family of four (with all the necessary adjustments for real income factored in) should be considered immoral. If we cannot learn to live on $250,000, we are an immoral people. Keeping more than $250,000 should be treated like having sex in public, watching pornography in front of children, or preparing and eating endangered species at the church potluck. It should be met with the "yuck factor" in moral deliberation.

When I read Smith's interesting piece, I immediately had two thoughts. First, this proposal cannot be recognized as anything but fantasy in the US as long as billionaires are treated like royalty, as if they are superintelligent persons who deserve our respect for being billionaires despite how they earned their money or how much or little they give away. Second, this proposal should be recognized by United Methodists as eminently sound because one of our normative doctrinal standards is John Wesley's sermon "On Riches." Wesley is much more rigorous than Smith. He states, "What a hindrance are riches to the very first fruit of faith, namely, the love of God." He defines the rich person as "anyone who possesses more than the necessaries and conveniences of life." Smith's proposal is much more lenient on us than Wesley.

In another sermon, "On the Use of Money," Wesley gives practical counsel to gain all we can, save all we can, and then give all we can. It is the latter that we have abandoned. Paul tells us that the reason we are sick and dying is due to income inequality where the rich humiliate those who have nothing by showing off what they have. To continue in this way is to have "contempt for the church" (1 Corinthians 11:22). Similarly, the first use of the term *church* in Acts is when "great fear" came upon it because Ananias and Sapphira refused to be accountable with their possessions. If we took up Smith's number of $250,000, a very high number that the vast majority of people of the world would consider exceedingly wealthy, as to what it is faithful to keep annually of one's income and created a church expectation that the remainder must be given away, then we could do something concrete about income inequality in our churches and in society. Perhaps we, as a global church, could create some kind of sovereign wealth fund that could do some of the work Bruenig noted above?

Although I think Smith's proposal has little chance in US society, I think there might be a church someday, one steeped in Scripture and attentive to the Holy Spirit, who could hear it; a church where at each annual charge conference every member is required to report what they earned that year and what they gave away, much as clergy do in our annual report. That money could go into a wealth fund to be dispensed by the whole church after discerning true needs in the local community. It could create structures of charity, so people could do something enjoyable with their lives rather than toil in misery. If you enjoy your work, work. If your work makes you miserable and unfree, perhaps it could set you free. It could break the power of wage labor that deadens the soul, turns people to addiction, and destroys families.

We do not have that church now, largely because the church has been absorbed by the US society and its market discipline. It cannot even raise a voice against the detention of innocent children at the border, so how could it begin to raise this question, one Wesley himself raised? Yet this should not prevent us from asking how to begin to lay foundations for that other church, one where this very modest proposal could be taken seriously; where church membership would be a function of a willingness to live on a "moral maximum income," and everything else would be given to the poor, to mental and physical health, to the arts, to education, to mission and more, and in the process, hopefully, we could overcome the curse of demeaning and arduous toil. For we should remember that hard and difficult labor, the kind of work most people do in the world today, is not rewarding; it is not a vocation. It is a curse (Genesis 3:17–19). Taking those curses upon himself, Jesus has redeemed us, even now, from those curses. We must find ways to show that redemption in our everyday lives by refusing to bow to cursed work. Recovering charity not as sentimental giving but as a social practice that redeems people from the curse of work through creating a culture of a "moral maximum income" is not radical, but it is a start. Although it has little chance at present, if the church begins to address its own income inequality, perhaps those in the state would see it is possible to do so without the fears many immediately raise when questions of economic equality emerge.

3. Third, we will also need to challenge the "warring madness" of the state. We cannot give our freedom over to generals and professional military leaders whose entire life has been formed by resolving social problems with violence. I mean no disrespect; nor do I intend to caricature. I have known professional military leaders who are less prone to resolve everything through war than hawkish politicians. They have seen war and its aftermath. Nonetheless, when your training and life are formed through the lens of war, you should expect warring to be a "natural" response to social ills. We should be concerned about a professional solider class that resents civilian life, whether they be military or police. As Juvenal wrote in the fourth century, "Quia custodiet ipsos custodes?" (Who will guard the guardians?). Even to raise this question, to take a knee during the playing of the national anthem in order to question the guardians who are entrusted with the execution of state violence, has, in large segments of our society, been successfully policed out of our cultural and political discussion. This policing should cause alarm.[23]

Much as the corporation needs democratizing, so does the military. How do we ensure that it has civilian control, that it serves

---

23 Radley Balko begins his sobering history of policing with Juvenal's quote. See the first chapter of *Rise of the Warrior Cop: The Militarization of America's Police Forces* (New York: Public Affairs, 2013).

the common good? One way to do so would be through universal conscription. If every eligible citizen had the possibility of executing the wars that the politicians deemed necessary, we might have a better political discussion about those wars. Perhaps we would at least need to figure out what the war is about and whether it is worthy of our, or our children's, lives. The resentment we see arising from a professional military class against nonmilitary citizens has some basis in the lack of shared burdens. As someone committed to nonviolence, I think universal conscription would also need to have exemptions for conscientious objectors and selective conscientious objectors, who would then need to do alternative service in difficult situations. Most statistics suggest that there are jobs such as lumberjacks, commercial fishing, roofing, power line workers, and others that have a higher death rate than combat. That is not to take away the somber reality of combat death, but it should put it in perspective. There are other important ways to serve society and learn courage. We could have a peace corps committed to building the housing units in urban areas Bruenig set forth as an interesting policy prescription.

Along with democratizing the military, the church must attend to mass incarceration, both by creating programs for the broken individuals who endure that system and the policies that make it possible. One place that lacks transparency and accountability is our prisons. Sometimes, truth itself is kept out. For instance, Florida and North Carolina banned adult prisoners from having access to Michelle Alexander's *The New Jim Crow.* New Jersey and New York attempted to do so but relented after protests.[24] Much as African Americans were not allowed to attend *The Birth of a Nation* in some cities for fear of race riots, so some prisoners are kept from attending to the conditions of their incarceration for similar reasons. The truth of our prisons must become better known. It is insufficient to evangelize captive audiences without attending to the social conditions that made them captive in the

---

24 Jonah Engel Bromich, "Why Are American Prisons So Afraid of This Book?," *New York Times,* January 18, 2018, https://www.nytimes.com /2018/01/18/us/new-jim-crow-book-ban-prison.html.

first place. Such a truncated mission would be akin to the exhortation from James, "If a brother or sister is naked and lacks daily food, and one of you says to them, 'Go in peace, keep warm and eat your fill,' and yet you do not supply their bodily needs, what is the good of that? So faith by itself, if it has no works, is dead" (James 2:15–17).

The Christian faith cannot be freely exercised if we cannot welcome the stranger. Here too there are complicated issues that should be addressed that the politics of fear prevent us from addressing because we have no reasonable discussion about immigration and refugee resettlement. The Trump GOP has demonstrated an utter lack of truthfulness on this issue. We need journalists and economists, social workers and clergy, to guide us into a better discussion. What fears are genuine? Who suffers, if they do, from migrant workers coming to this country? What is our role in the refugee crisis from the consequences of our wars? If we broke it, do we not need to fix it?

My second and third points above could suggest that I have repeated rather than avoided what I laid out in my first point. The first point suggested that the virtue of truth telling required broadening the conversation beyond that of the politicians and warriors of the state or the wealthy businesspeople of the market. More attention should be given to those forms of life that make us truly human, which are not government and commerce. Yet I focused in the second point on economics and in the third on the state. Did I not give attention to the very forms of life that I suggested needed less attention? In response, I would say that I did so to question, not reassert, their dominance over our ethical, cultural, and political imagination. How might we think about our common life together, so that something other than the dominating roles of the politician, warrior, and businessperson are always before us? Journalism could help us here, but too many journalists chase these characters much more than is necessary and neglect all the other more humanizing persons and characters available to them. The university matters here. As a professor who sits on university committees, I'm often struck by how the university works, bringing together diverse nations, religions, cultures in a search for wisdom. I often desire that the church look more like the university. Likewise, we need a noncommercial commitment to art, sport, and other activities that we pursue outside of any profit motive. It is in these places that we learn to tell the truth.

When I teach ethics, I often take students through the variety of ethical theories available and then ask them if their parents, friends, clergy, band teacher, coach, or some other significant person in their life taught them these theories and how to use them so they could be ethical. I have never (thanks be to God) had a student answer that question affirmatively. I then follow it up by questioning whether they can then truly claim to know anything about ethics, about what is true and good. They all think that they do—and I seldom doubt them. The next logical question is, From whom did you get this knowledge? Whatever the answer is to that question, whichever person, author, community, organization, activity, taught you to tell the truth, to say of what is that it is and of what is not that it is not, that is the place we need to look, strengthen, and preserve to remember that it is truth and not power that is the condition for freedom. Whatever person, author, community, organization, activity tried to convince you to say of what is that it is not and of what is not that it is—flee, for that is what you should rightly fear.

Will truth telling set us free? It cannot do so without the virtues of courage, faith, and hope. Truth telling appeared not to work out so well for Socrates, Jesus, Martin Luther King Jr., John Brown, and countless others, but where would we be if we did not have their truth telling? History is littered with those whose truth telling did not free them but whose witness to the truth was nonetheless the condition for our freedom, for our courage to deliberate about what is good and true. We tell the truth not because we

> Truth telling appeared not to work out so well for Socrates, Jesus, Martin Luther King Jr., John Brown, and countless others, but where would we be if we did not have their truth telling?

are convinced it will have an immediate impact, but because we have faith that this is how God builds God's reign. Telling the truth witnesses to our hope. Because it witnesses to hope, truth telling can be something more than an appeal for power. Truth telling can dare to be charitable, seeking not to win or destroy but to live consistently with the image of God in which we are made. Truth and charity are God's very nature. What greater reason could there be for their importance?

INDEX

CPSIA information can be obtained
at www.ICGtesting.com
Printed in the USA
LVHW091151100919

630510LV00001B/5/P

9 781945 935503